Explorations
in Musical
Materials

Explorations in Musical Materials

a working approach to making music

JAMES YANNATOS

Harvard University

Prentice-Hall, Inc., Englewood Cliffs, N.J. 07632

Library of Congress Cataloging in Publication Data

Yannatos, James.
   Explorations in musical materials.

   Includes bibliographies and index.
    1. Music—Theory. 2. Composition (Music)
I. Title.
MT40.Y36   781   77-20166
ISBN 0-13-295956-9

© 1978 by Prentice-Hall, Inc., Englewood Cliffs, N.J. 07632

Printed in the United States of America

10 9 8 7 6 5 4 3 2 1

Prentice-Hall International, Inc., *London*
Prentice-Hall of Australia Pty. Limited, *Sydney*
Prentice-Hall of Canada, Ltd., *Toronto*
Prentice-Hall of India Private Limited, *New Delhi*
Prentice-Hall of Japan, Inc., *Tokyo*
Prentice-Hall of Southeast Asia Pte. Ltd., *Singapore*
Whitehall Books Limited, *Wellington, New Zealand*

781
Yau

CONTENTS

PREFACE

This book was developed during three years of teaching elementary composition. Because many of the students knew little music, we began with the most basic elements of music. The Harvard undergraduates learned musical vocabulary as they explored the shapes and sounds of music. This exploration involved their feelings and intuitions toward music and made their study of "the tradition" more meaningful as they worked with the exercises. Each exercise whether dealing with simple sounds or complex arrangements of sounds—was a discovery for the student and for me.

When teachers reexamine the elements of music with the fresh perspective and perceptions of their students, they can better organize their own understanding of basic musical elements—no matter what period of music they specialize in. The exercises, projects, listening suggestions, analyses, and questions in the various chapters are meant to create such a deepened understanding by student and teacher.

I would like to thank my own students for their curiosity, interest, and excitement. Particular thanks are due to Martin Robbins, who enthusiastically edited the manuscript and made many useful suggestions; to Richard St. Clair, for his devotion and valuable assistance in reading and correcting the manuscript; to Nyia, my wife, who read the various versions of the manuscript with her astute, critical eye; and to Dion, Kalya, and Nyia, for their continuing support and patience.

INTRODUCTION

This book is an introductory text in basic musicianship, theory, and composition. It provides a broad survey of musical materials for the student training to be a musician—whether as a teacher, performer, or composer—and is a comprehensive introduction for the nonprofessional who is curious about music and its creation.

The book is divided into four sections, which deal, respectively, with sound, space, time, and their integration. Each section develops specific elements of music (tone, intervals, and so forth).

Chapters 5–8, which deal with the vocabulary of *intervals* and *chords*, should prepare the student for the subsequent chapters in the book that treat the elements of time, melody, and harmony.

The book's unique features include sections that introduce the student to polytonal, atonal, twelve-tone, and aleatoric materials and techniques used in today's expanded musical language while relating these to the more traditional materials and techniques of the past.

The book explores musical materials through exercises and very short compositional projects. Step by step, the student works with musical materials, starting from a freer usage of sound and working towards progressively greater degrees of control. This approach helps prepare the student to *hear, understand, use,* and *control* the expanded vocabulary of contemporary music and relate it to the music of the past. Ear training is an integral part of this approach.

Student compositions are equally important to individual and class development. They should be performed in class whenever possible so that they can be heard and discussed. The music suggested for listening and analysis that relates to specific problems should also be examined and performed whenever possible.

The approach of this text stresses writing and correcting, playing and singing, listening and analyzing. This book differs basically from texts that begin with examples of existing music—"the tradition." To categorize, analyze, listen to, and appreciate such examples is certainly useful. But that approach often intimidates students with the past's achievements. Worse, it eliminates the most important element of learning—the student's creative initiative.

From the beginning, students should involve their own feelings in organizing the basic elements of music into short exercises and compositions. The writing of music, no matter how short or simple, is an exciting creative experience. It is also a more direct way of learning how music is put together. Performance, listening, and analyzing can then give deeper insights into the music that is being learned firsthand.

Learning is a total process. The overall goal of this book is to involve the student in making music—both writing it and performing it. Because music is best learned by making it, this book encourages students to write and perform their own music as they expand their knowledge of the materials of music. They will then better recognize and understand the musical materials available to all composers.

Because this book is not limited to an examination of the traditional styles in historical sequence, students will work with many styles. This should make them less hesitant to express their own ideas and explore their own potentialities. The results of this exploration will be appreciated by the students as they become better listeners and more aware musicians. They will have taken their *own* first steps in understanding music.

This text can be used in many ways. First, it can accommodate a particular musical emphasis—composition, theory, musicianship, or music appreciation. Second, it can be adapted to class level and size. Third, the examples, exercises, projects, analyses, and listening suggestions can be adapted and enlarged at the teacher's initiative, based on musical emphasis and on class needs. Finally, the teacher can alter the sequence of chapters depending on the subject and on the level and the size of the class. For example, the teacher could begin with the more traditional elements of music (intervals and chords), as presented in Chapters 5–8, while introducing one or two exercises from Chapter 1 in order to engage the class immediately in newer modes of musical thought. Notation is introduced in Chapter 2 so that students can deal with various aspects of their musical exploration.

Musical examples (piano or piano reductions) should be played by the student. Records may be substituted for those examples not originally composed for piano; this way, the student may gain a more accurate sense of the actual sound.

Exercises and *projects* allow the student to sing individually, or with his classmates, various musical examples. Thus, whatever instrument the student plays can be incorporated. With the teacher's help, students should perform their compositional projects in *informal concerts*. Such concerts encourage performance and generate student enthusiasm and appreciation for one another's work. Many exercises can be done at home as well as in the classroom by anyone interested in learning more about music.

The *listening suggestions* and problems of *musical analysis* that occur at various points in the book expand particular problems posed in the exercises and projects.

Each chapter is prefaced by one or more *objectives* and a list of *capsule definitions.* These short definitions are expanded in the subsequent discussion, examples, and exercises. The *bibliography* at the end of each section lists supplementary books that the student may use to research various aspects of the text.

*Explorations
in Musical
Materials*

1 *Sound*

1 SOUND:
Environmental and Musical

OBJECTIVES

1. To *examine* various *kinds* of sound found in the *environment* and made by *instruments*.

2. To *recognize* the different *qualities* of percussion instruments.

3. To *use* various sounds as musical materials.

CAPSULE DEFINITIONS

Sound	In practical terms, anything you can hear.
Noise	"Confused" sound.
Frequency	Pitch.
Dissonance	"Harsh," "tense" sound, or pitches that clash.
Quality	Tone color (timbre).
Texture	Density (thickness or thinness of sound).
Intensity	Dynamics (loud or soft, forte or piano).
Duration	The length of a sound.
Attack	The start of a sound.
Decay	The end of a sound.
Style	A particular way in which music is organized.

A. Basic Notions of Sound

"If music be the food of love"—then *sound* is the food of music. Without it, we could not "play on."

Sound is the basic building material for music. It is all around us— in the rustling of the leaves moved by the wind, in a baby's laugh, in dishes being stacked. Each sound holds rich associations and affects us in particular ways. The trip to the woods or the ocean is a change from one set of sounds to another.

Each sound moves. Once it is set in motion, it changes its character constantly until it disappears. Sound happens in real *space* and *time*. A sound needs space and time in order to be heard as a sound.

Claude Debussy said that "sounds in any combination and in any succession" could be used in music.[1] John Cage advocates a music which is open "to the sounds . . . in the environment,"[2] thereby enlarging Debussy's notion of music to include environmental sounds.

Sound, as it has been understood and used by composers, has changed throughout history. Bach, Beethoven, Debussy, and Schoenberg *sound* differently. Each composer used the same twelve tones, but put them together in different ways. The *way* composers combined tones into chords and melodies, and the musical forms that evolved, resulted in a variety of musical *styles* throughout history.

Today, the notion of sound encompasses a variety of nontraditional sounds, including *nonpitched sounds* (sounds without recognizable pitch) from the electronic, tape, environmental, instrumental and vocal mediums and *pitched sounds* (tones, intervals, and chords), as well as new ways of putting these sounds together. Since "sounds in any combination and in any succession" can be used in a piece of music, we are free to choose those sounds from among the many that could function as possible musical material.

But a sound by itself is not music. Sounds by themselves need a composer's guiding ear and hand in order to become sounds in space and time and thereby to function as music.

Many composers have had difficulty having their music accepted as music. Many critics have disagreed with composers as to what music is.

[1] John Cage, *Silence* (Cambridge, Mass.: M. I. T. Press, 1969) p. 68.
[2] Cage, *Silence,* p. 8.

To some critics, music that sounded new, harsh, or dissonant to their ears was ugly and therefore questionable as music.

EXERCISE 1-1

    A   Listen to the Overture to Beethoven's opera *Fidelio*.

    B   Read the following review, written in 1806:

Recently, there was given the Overture to Beethoven's opera *Fidelio*, and all impartial musicians and music lovers were in perfect agreement that never was anything as incoherent, shrill, chaotic and ear-splitting produced in music. The most piercing dissonances clash in a really atrocious harmony, and a few puny ideas only increase the disagreeable and deafening effect.[3]

    C   Do you agree with the critic? Why? Why not?

    D   What do you think the critic meant by "incoherent, shrill, chaotic and ear-splitting"?

    E   What could he have meant by "piercing *dissonances* clash in a really atrocious *harmony*"?

EXERCISE 1-2

    A   Listen to Debussy's *L'Après-Midi d'un Faune*.

    B   Read the following review, written in 1904:

Debussy's *L'Après-Midi d'un Faune* was a strong example of modern ugliness. . . . The work gives as much dissonance as any of the most modern art works in music.[4]

    C   Do you agree with the critic? Why? Why not?

    D   What do you think the critic meant by "modern ugliness. . . . much dissonance"?

RESULTS   Each of the composers lived at a different time, spoke a different language, and used the sounds available to him. Each put those sounds together in ways unique to himself and his time. The musical result in each case was quite different.

The critic in each case seemed unfamiliar with the *language* of the piece he heard. The sounds of the piece and the ways the composer organized them appeared "shrill, chaotic and ear-splitting."

[3] Nicolas Slonimsky, *Lexicon of Musical Invective* (New York: Coleman Press Co., 1965) p. 42.

[4] Slonimsky, *Lexicon*, p. 92.

Unlike the critic, we should keep an open ear and mind to sound and its many uses.

B. Basic Properties of Sound

No matter where we live, we are surrounded by *sound*. Some sounds are pleasant, others are not. A sound can be a *single*, identifiable sound, or a combination of many sounds—a *composite* sound. A sound can be loud or soft, high or low.

EXERCISE 1-3

Think of the various sounds you hear throughout the day.

A   List some of these sounds.
B   Which are single sounds. Which are composite sounds?
C   Which sounds are Loud? Soft? High? Low?
D   Which of these sounds recur often?
E   Which sounds are pleasant? Which unpleasant? Why?
    (Is the distinction related to their loud or soft, high or low, or repetitive character?)
F   Which sounds would you describe as noise? Why?

All sounds, pleasant or unpleasant, single or composite, loud or soft, high or low, have certain *common properties:*

1   Each sound is activated by a *sound source,* which can be as varied as a car engine starting, a baby crying, and a violin playing.
2   Each sound then moves in space from the sound source to a *receiver,* which could be a microphone or a human being.
3   Each sound has a *pitch* (high or low), which is dependent on its *frequency,* or the number of times per second the sound (in the form of *sound waves*) moves or vibrates. Some composite sounds are so complex that no specific pitch can be identified; these can be called nonpitched sounds.
4   Each sound lasts a certain length of time. The *duration* of a sound begins with the *attack,* which activates the sound, and ends with the *decay* of the sound. From attack to decay, the sound constantly changes its *character* or *quality* as the *intensity* of the sound changes.
5   Each sound has a certain *intensity* or *dynamic* level, which defines its degree of softness or loudness.
6   The sound properties of frequency, intensity, and duration contribute to the *density* or *texture* of the composite sound.

Among the many sounds available to a composer today, we will begin our exploration with single percussion sounds and other instrumental sounds. We will attempt to determine both the *sound* of each instrument and the effect of *dynamics* on the quality, duration, and pitch of each sound.

The following three exercises are limited by the choice of musical elements. Listen to the *sound* of each exercise, making your observations at the conclusion of the exercises.

EXERCISE 1-4

Play a single sound on any available percussion instrument, such as cymbals, wood blocks, timpani, any drum, bells, xylophone, and triangle. Use different types of *beaters,* such as mallets and sticks made of different materials, and different kinds of *strokes,* such as hit and rubbed.

A. Play each of the various available instruments loudly (forte) and softly (piano).

B. Repeat A, but use different mallets or sticks.

C. Describe each percussion instrument in regard to its:

1. *character* or *quality* of sound.

2. *quality* of sound as it is affected by the type of beater (stick or mallet), the kind of stroke (hit or rubbed), and the dynamic level (piano or forte).

3. general *register* (high or low).

4. *pitch* as it is affected by the stick or mallet, the kind of stroke, and the dynamic level.

5. *duration,* or sustaining power, as it is affected by the stick or mallet, the kind of stroke, and the dynamic level.

If no percussion instruments are available, substitute percussionlike instruments, such as a pot cover, a desk, and hands.

Sound includes the various "effects" that can be produced by instruments. There are various ways to produce an "effect." One could *pluck* or *hit* a string on a string instrument or inside a piano, play on or behind the bridge of a stringed instrument, or use the wood of a bow to hit a string. One could blow a wind or brass instrument without making an actual tone, or could *overblow,* the tongue fluttering on the roof of the mouth to produce a *flutter* tone. Or a person could hit the pads, keys, or mouthpiece of an instrument with fingers or hand to produce a snapping percussive sound.

EXERCISE 1-5

Experiment with the instrument you play to create *new* sounds.

A. Play each sound loudly (forte) and quickly, and then softly (piano) and slowly, holding the sound.
B. Repeat A, but reverse the dynamics.
C. Describe each instrument in regard to its:
1. general *character* or *quality* of sound.
2. *quality* of sound as it is affected by dynamic, stroke, and duration.
3. general *register* (high and/or low).
4. *pitch* as it is affected by dynamic, stroke, and duration.

EXERCISE 1-6

Substituting vowel ("ah," "oh," "ee," etc.) and consonant ("d," "p," "k," etc.) vocal sounds for sustained and short sounds, imitate the sound of the various percussion instruments played in Exercise 1-4 or the instrumental sounds produced in Exercise 1-5.

RESULTS   Many of the instrumental and vocal "effects" do *not* have a *specific pitch*. But many of these sounds can be identified by *register*. Some instruments sustain a sound *longer* than others (cymbals longer than a wood block, for instance). *Dynamics* (the intensity of the stroke) and the type of beater or stick (mallet, bow, and so on) affect the *duration*, the *quality*, and the *pitch* of a sound from its *attack* to its *decay*. This creates a sense of *motion* within the sound as it changes. The changing sound also moves in real space from the instrument or voice to the ear that hears it. Music requires both types of motion.

To Sum Up   Sound includes both environmental and musical sounds produced in a variety of ways. Each sound has a beginning and an end, an attack and a decay during which the *quality* of the sound changes. Each sound, single or composite, pitched or nonpitched, can be loud or soft, can be high or low, and can last a certain duration, depending on what produced it and how it was produced.

PROJECT 1-1

Listen to the various sounds that you hear each day—on the street, in the classroom, in the dining hall and elsewhere. Record them, if you have a tape recorder; list them if you do not. Describe each sound in terms of its *intensity* (loudness or softness), *quality* (high or low frequencies), *texture* (density: thickness or thinness), and the characteristics that make it a pleasant or unpleasant sound.

PROJECT 1-2

Go to a busy intersection and record the various sounds you hear.

A   *Edit* the tape, isolating particular sound combinations from others.
B   *Re-record* some of these sections—at half speed, double speed, and backwards.
C   *Combine* them in different ways to produce a collage of sounds. Strive for variety of intensity, quality, and texture.

PROJECT 1-3

Record the "effects" you produced in Exercise 1-5. Arrange them as in Project 1-2.

LISTENING
SUGGESTIONS

Beethoven: *Fidelio* Overture
Debussy: *L'Après-Midi d'un Faune*
Cage: *Fontana Mix*

Describe the different sounds each composer uses and the types of instruments used to produce the sounds.

2 SOUND: Pitched and Nonpitched

OBJECTIVES

1. To *examine* various kinds of vocal and instrumental sound.

2. To *explore* simple forms of motion and texture.

3. To *use* these sounds with the elements of dynamics, tempo, duration, and silence to create simple forms of musical motion, texture, and shape-form.

CAPSULE DEFINITIONS

Register	General pitch areas (low, medium, high).
Frequency spectrum	The frequencies from high to low.
Range	Distance from lowest to highest sounds (pitched or nonpitched).
Pitch	Periodic wave-form with a specific frequency (in vibrations per second) or an identifiable tone (A, B, and so on).
Nonpitched sound	Sound with no discernible pitch.
Timbre	The tone color or quality of a sound.
Tempo	Time, rate of movement, or speed.
Shape-form	The form of a piece as it evolves.
Musical elements	Melody, harmony, rhythm, texture, timbre.
Dynamics	Forte—loud (f).
	Piano—soft (p).
	Mezzo forte—medium loud (mf).
	Mezzo piano—medium soft (mp).
	Crescendo (cresc.)—getting louder (———).
	Diminuendo (dim.)—getting softer (———).
Duration	The length of sound; long or short.

A. Preliminary Explorations

The concept of musically acceptable sounds has been broadened in the twentieth century to include environmental as well as musical sounds. These sounds range from *pitched* sounds, which have a specific frequency and a name such as A, B, C, to *nonpitched* sounds, whose frequencies are wide-ranging and too complex to be specified.

Some single and composite nonpitched sounds can be identified by register (high or low). Others, ranging from random noise to multi-frequency sounds, are too confused to be heard in terms of register. These multi-frequency sounds, however, can create a "spread" texture that extends through one or more registers.

EXERCISE 2-1

Listen to and look at various examples of twentieth-century music chosen by your teacher from the following list :

Stockhausen: *Gesange der Junglinge*
Penderecki: *Threnody*
Crumb: *Ancient Voices of Children*
Ligeti: *Aventures*
Bartók: *Music for Strings, Percussion, and Celesta*
Husa: *Music from Prague—1968*
Schoenberg: *Five Pieces for Orchestra*

QUESTIONS AND
OBSERVATIONS

1   Which composers used pitched sounds? Which used nonpitched sounds? Which used a combination of pitched and nonpitched sounds?

2   Could you detect any relationship between the *sounds* the composers imagined and the *symbols* they wrote?

3   How would you describe the texture of each example?

As you listen to the examples above, you should be aware of the many different sounds that combine in various ways to create a musical *texture*. You might describe this texture as thin, transparent, thick, or dense. In some examples, the distinction between pitched and nonpitched sounds becomes blurred when specific pitches cannot be heard because of the very dense texture.

11

B. Musical Motion

While listening to music, you should be aware of the *texture* and the *motion* that is created as sounds combine and change. *Musical motion* is generated when one sound moves to other sounds in succession. A single sound moving in real space creates a simple form of musical motion as its sound changes in intensity.

In Exercises 2-2–2-4 single percussion and vocal nonpitched sounds will be used in succession with varied dynamics and duration to create musical motion. Since we are using sounds without specific pitch, a simpler form of notation, one that utilizes graph paper rather than music paper, will be adequate. Each square represents one second of time. The *duration* of a sound can then be notated by drawing a line from left to right through the appropriate number of squares:

Dynamics can be notated *under* the sound. In addition to forte and piano, dynamic levels include *mezzo forte* (*mf*), *mezzo piano* (*mp*), *crescendo (cresc.* ———), and *diminuendo* (————). A loud, high sound held for four seconds followed by a soft, low sound held for two seconds that increased in loudness and in pitch for five seconds could be notated as follows:

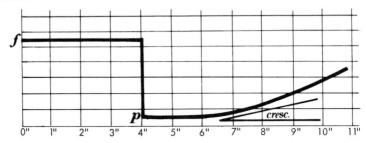

Exercises 2-2–2-4 are limited by their choice of musical elements, but each has musical possibilities. Listen to the *sound* and judge the *effect* of each exercise, making your observations at the conclusion of the exercises. Notate each exercise when appropriate. Vary your position in relation to the sound source in order to hear the effect of the sound from different places.

EXERCISE 2-2

Choose a single percussion instrument and an appropriate stick or mallet.

12

A. Play a sound forte, then piano two seconds later.

B. Repeat A, but extend the exercise to ten seconds, alternating the forte and piano sounds every two seconds. Notate it.

C. Repeat B, but extend the exercise to twelve seconds, alternating the forte and piano every three seconds. Notate it.

D. Vary B or C in the following ways:

1. Use a different stick or mallet.

2. Use a different percussion instrument.

3. Let each forte sound ring, and dampen each piano sound.

4. Reverse 3.

E. Repeat B–D, substituting a vocal or instrumental nonpitched sound (vowel, consonant, or "effect") for the percussion sound.

F. Repeat B–D, alternating a vocal nonpitched sound (vowel, consonant) or another instrumental effect (hitting pads of flute or playing on the bridge of the violin, etc.).

QUESTIONS AND
OBSERVATIONS

1 If the *effect* of a piece of music is dependent on the *variety* of its sound and the *motion* its sound generates, which of exercises B–E is most effective? Why?

2 Which of exercises B–E is least effective? Why?

3 Cound you improve Exercise 2-2? How?

4 Revise Exercise 2-2 accordingly. Play it. Is it more effective now?

EXERCISE 2-3

Write variations of Exercise 2-2, B–F that are *not* included in your revision.

A. Reverse the dynamics.

B. Alter the dynamics.

C. Alter the duration.

D. Extend the exercise.

E. Combine any of A–D.

F. Notate A through E:

EXERCISE 2-4

A Write a ten-to-fifteen-second piece. Combine any vocal and instrumental sounds. Use varied *dynamics* and *duration* to generate musical motion.

B Use additional vocal and instrumental sounds that will make your piece more *varied* but still *coherent*.

Compare these versions with those in Exercises 2-2 and 2-3.

QUESTIONS AND
OBSERVATIONS

1   Which are more interesting?
2   By using additional sounds, how could you improve the earlier versions to heighten the sense of *musical motion*? Revise these versions accordingly. Play them. Are they more "effective" now?

As more sounds are combined with the elements of duration and dynamics, more varied pieces can be written. Although these combined elements can help create a greater sense of musical motion, more care must be given to their organization into a coherent shape-form.

To Sum Up   A simple form of musical motion can be generated by a single sound that is repeated, but at the same time varied by the altering of *dynamics* and *duration*. However, for a greater sense of musical motion to be created, a sound followed by *different* sounds (pitched or non-pitched) with the same or varied dynamics, duration, and instrumentation is needed.

C. Musical Texture

Whereas musical motion is an aspect of musical time, musical texture is an aspect of musical space. Sounds that are combined spread "up or down" over the various registers to create *musical texture*.

There are many ways of combining sounds to create texture:

1   A sound can be *doubled* by other voices or instruments:

2   One sound can *overlap* another sound:

3   Different sounds can be *superimposed*:

4   Superimposed sounds can *alternate* with a single, doubled, or overlapping sound:

In Exercises 2-5–2-9 nonpitched vocal sounds will be used to create a simple form of musical texture as well as a limited form of musical motion. Again, we can use graph paper for notation, since we are using sounds distinguished by *register* rather than by *specific pitch*.

Register is represented by the squares from bottom to top, each square representing a slightly higher pitch area. If a sound spreads beyond a particular register, more squares should be filled in. For example:

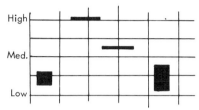

Exercises 2-5–2-8 are to be done as a class improvisation of approximately ten seconds. Each is limited by its choice of musical materials, but each has musical possibilities.

Listen to both the *sound* and the *effect* of each exercise, making your observations at the appropriate time.

EXERCISE 2-5

A. By yourself, sustain the vocal sound "sh."
B. Repeat A, with one or more of your classmates.
C. Repeat B, with all your classmates.
D. Repeat A, but start with your classmates in the front of the class being joined gradually by all your classmates.
E. Repeat D, but start with your classmates in the back of the class being joined gradually by all your classmates.
F. Notate A through E.

Texture can be affected and modified by (1) *dynamics,* which intensify (f, ◁————) or lighten (p, ————▷) the texture; and (2) *time,* in the form of *tempo,* which regulates the speed or rate of change of the texture. In each case, the *quality* of the texture will be altered.

EXERCISE 2-6

Repeat Exercise 2-5, D–E, using the following dynamics:

A   Piano (soft).
B   Forte (loud).

C   Piano ——*cresc.* forte, with each additional entrance of your classmates louder than the previous one.

D   Forte *dim.*—— piano, with each additional entrance of your classmates softer than the previous one.

E   Piano ——= forte =—— piano.

F   Notate E.

EXERCISE 2-7

Repeat Exercise 2-6, A–E, using the following tempos:

A   Slow to fast, with each additional entrance of your classmates
slightly sooner than the previous one.

B   Fast to slow, with each additional entrance of your classmates slightly
later than the previous one.

C   Notate A or B.

QUESTIONS AND
OBSERVATIONS

1   What is the general effect of the doubling and overlapping of the
"sh" sound?

2   What is the effect on the texture of the changes in dynamics? Of the
changes in tempo?

3   Was there any sense of pitch or pitch variation in the different versions? Describe.

4   Which versions were most varied and interesting? Which were least
varied and interesting? Why?

5   Did you get a sense of musical motion as well as of changing texture?
Describe.

6   Do you think your reaction to the sound, motion, and texture would
be different if you sat in another place in the room?

RESULTS

In Exercise 2-5, the piling up and movement of the "sh" sound
causes a thickening of texture. The movement of the "sh" from one place
to another gives the impression of a diminuendo or crescendo, for
the sound appears to be approaching or receding, depending upon the
hearer's position.

In Exercises 2-6 and 2-7, increases in speed and dynamics thicken
the texture; decreases in speed and dynamics thin the texture.

EXERCISE 2-8

Take the least interesting version(s) from Exercises 2-5, 2-6, and
2-7, and revise it. As more sounds are combined with the elements of
tempo and dynamics, more varied and interesting textures can be
created.

Exercise 2-9, which calls for voices and instruments, combines two or more sounds that are varied by tempo and dynamics. Listen for those sounds that emerge from the texture, as opposed to other sounds that seem less important.

EXERCISE 2-9

A Write a ten-to-fifteen-second piece based on Exercise 2-5, 2-6, or 2-7 to be performed by you and your classmates. Use two or more vocal sounds (vowel or consonant) varied by tempo and dynamics.

B Repeat A, but substitute short and long percussion or quasi-percussion sounds (for instance, tapped and clapped sounds) for the vocal sounds.

C Use both vocal and instrumental sounds (including percussion or quasi-percussion sounds) to write a new version of A.

QUESTIONS AND OBSERVATIONS

1 What is the general effect of the contrasting vocal and instrumental sounds.

2 What is the effect on the texture of dynamics? Tempo? Instrumentation (vocal and instrumental sounds)?

3 Did you get a sense of musical motion as well as of changing texture? Describe?

4 Did some sounds appear more important than others? Why?

5 Did any of the versions have a sense of order and coherence—that is, a shape-form? Why? Why not?

D. Shape-Form

No matter how hard it is to describe the precise shape-form of a piece, the success of the piece depends upon the sense of *order* and *coherence* the listener perceives as shape-form. The choice of musical materials, the way they are put together, the texture and motion that result—all contribute to the shape-form as it evolves. The most beautiful musical idea, if not put together well, can lead nowhere. On the other hand, the most banal musical fragment, if embodied in a coherent shape-form, can become a meaningful composition.

EXERCISE 2-10

A Listen to Example 2-1.

B Describe the composer's use of pitched and nonpitched sounds in relation to *dynamics* and *tempo*.

C Describe the composer's use of vowel and consonant sounds in relation to *pitch, dynamics,* and *tempo.*

Example 2-1.   **Crumb:** *Ancient Voices of Children* (two excerpts)

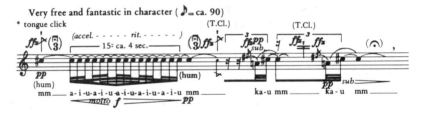

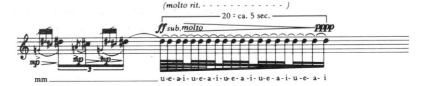

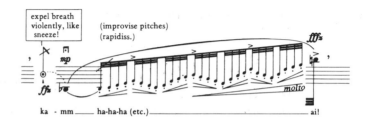

D   What is the range of each excerpt?

E   Does each excerpt hold together as a whole and create a sense of musical motion?

To be successful, a piece must be perceived as a *whole*. The musical materials, by their elaboration and development, move through changing textures, and the result of this movement is a unique shape-form.

EXERCISE 2-11

Refer to Exercises 2-5 through 2-8.

A   In which exercises did you perceive a shape-form?

B   Choose an exercise in which you could not perceive a shape-form. What would you do to improve it? Write your revised version.

E. Silence

The composer John Cage asks, "Is there such a thing as silence? Is there always something to hear, never any peace and quiet?" [1]

[1] John Cage, *Silence*, p. 42.

EXERCISE 2-12

Remain silent for 30 to 60 seconds.

A   Describe the quality of that silence.
B   Does silence have its own sound?
C   Would you consider silence a sound element that can be used in music? If so, how could it be used?

EXERCISE 2-13

Select any one of Exercises 2-5 through 2-8 that you notated.

A   Introduce the element of silence at various points throughout the exercise.
B   Copy it on the blackboard and have it performed by your classmates.
C   How does your use of silence affect the *motion*, the *texture*, and the *shape-form* of the piece?

EXERCISE 2-14

Take any piece you have heard and/or examined.

A   Does the composer use silence in his piece?
B   Does he use silence often? Rarely?
C   What effect is produced by his use of silence?

Silence, understood as the absence of sound, does not have any specific frequency, but it can act as a textural element that complements sound. T. S. Eliot wrote:

> Words, after speech, reach
> Into the silence. Only by the form, the pattern,
> Can words or music reach
> The stillness, as a Chinese jar still
> Moves perpetually in its stillness.[2]

To Sum Up   We may consider a silence in a conversation, or in music, to be an example of Eliot's "felt silence"—something that is *felt* more strongly than a mere absence of sound.

Both silence and sound contribute to the texture and motion that result in a shape-form. Musical texture is created by:

1   A single sound *doubled* by additional instruments and/or voices.

[2] T.S. Eliot, "Burnt Norton," in *Four Quartets*, (New York: Harcourt Brace Jovanovich, Inc.). Reprinted by permission of the publisher.

2   Many different sounds played and/or sung together as a composite sound.

3   Silence.

Each sound is affected by *dynamics, tempo,* and *instrumentation.*

Musical texture and musical motion contribute to the shape-form of a piece as it evolves.

PROJECT 2-1

Create a 15-to-30-second piece by introducing the element of *silence* into any exercise(s) in Chapters 1 and 2.

PROJECT 2-2

Using vocal and/or nonvocal sounds and silence, create a "new" piece. (Use graph paper and/or music paper.)

PROJECT 2-3

Find various implements to hit or rub as percussion instruments. Using the same *time* and *pitch* values from any exercise or project in Chapter 1 or 2 write a 15-to-30-second piece. You may add vocal sounds of different durations and dynamics. These sounds can either vary in pitch or lack pitch. (Indicate dynamics—[*f p mf mp*]—below the sounds. Keep in mind the sound elements that are most important in the evolving shape-form.)

PROJECT 2-4

Take any exercise in Chapter 2. Write a free 15-to-30-second piece, expanding your material so that it evolves into a coherent shape-form.

LISTENING SUGGESTIONS

Keep in mind the basic *sound element(s)* of the following pieces (pitched sounds, nonpitched sounds, and/or silence) and the *motion, texture,* and *shape-form* that results as the sounds move in *time* and through *space,* from sound source (record player) to you, the receiver.

Berio: *Sequenza III*
Stockhausen: *Gesang der Junglinge*
Street Cries of Charleston (History of Classical Jazz, Riverside SDP 11)
Haydn: *Symphony No. 104,* second movement
Varèse: *Ionisation*

3 PITCHED SOUND: The Tone

OBJECTIVES

1. To *examine* various kinds of pitched sounds—vocal and instrumental.
2. To *recognize* the *qualities* of tone produced by voices and instruments.

CAPSULE DEFINITIONS

Voiced sound	Pitched vocal sound.
Pitch	Periodic wave-form with a specific frequency (in vibrations per second).
Tone	Pitch with quality (i.e., color or timbre).
Overtones	"Extra" tones generated with the fundamental or main tones; also called harmonics or upper partials.
Overtone series	The fundamental and its overtones.
Overtone envelope	The number and intensity of upper partials included in the tone.
Register	General pitch areas (low, medium, high).
Range	Distance from lowest to highest tones used in a piece.
Contour	Shape of a melodic line.
Shape-form	The form of a piece as it evolves.
Instrumentation	Choice of instruments used to play music.

A. Preliminary Explorations

Although the concept of musically acceptable sounds has been broadened in the twentieth century to include nonpitched as well as pitched sound, much music written today is still based essentially, if not exclusively, on pitched sound. For the composers of this music, traditional forms of notation, sometimes combined with the more recent developments in notation, are adequate.

Pre-twentieth-century Western music is concerned predominantly with pitched sound. The variety of music that has been created with pitched sounds is astonishing. Thus, to gain a more comprehensive understanding of sound, we must include pitched sound in our study of musical materials.

EXERCISE 3-1

Listen and look at various examples of pre-twentieth-century music chosen by your teacher from the following list:

Christmas Cycle (Gregorian plainchant)
Leonin: *Judaea Jerusalem*
Perotin: *Sederunt Principes*
Gesualdo: *Dolcissima Mia Vita*
J. S. Bach: *Brandenberg Concerto No. 3*
Mozart: *Symphony No. 40*, first movement
Beethoven: *Fidelio* Overture
Debussy: *L'Après-Midi d'un Faune*

QUESTIONS AND
OBSERVATIONS

1 What was the basic musical material the composer used—simple tones, intervals, or chords?
2 What was the general range of each example—high, medium, or low?
3 Could you make out the relationship between the *sounds* the composer imagined and the *symbols* the composer wrote?
4 How would you describe the texture of each example?
5 Did you get a sense of the shape-form of each piece?

As you listen to the various examples, note the many different sounds—tones, intervals, and chords—that combine to generate musical motion, create a musical texture, and shape the piece. These sounds can range from very low to very high. To distinguish these pitched sounds, however, requires a precise way to *measure, name,* and *notate* them.

B. Notation: Pitched Sounds

There are twelve different pitches, each of which can be repeated in other *registers* (low, medium, or high) throughout the *range* of sound. Each pitch has a specific frequency—that is, a specific number of cycles (or vibrations) per second. Middle C (c^1) has a frequency of 262 cps (cycles per second). The C above middle C (c^2) has a frequency of 524 cps, or *double* the number of vibrations per second of c^1. The C below middle C (c) has a frequency of 131 cps, or *half* the number of vibrations per second of c^1.

Each pitch can be notated to show its high or low position in any register throughout the range. Middle C (c^1) can serve as the connecting link between high and low registers.

The five lines *above* and *below* c^1 are called the *great staff*. The clef above c^1 is called the *G clef* (𝄞), the clef below c^1 is called the *F clef* (𝄢). Lines can be added to the great staff in either direction for the purpose of notating very high or very low pitches.

The pitches between c^1 and c^2 are designated d^1, e^1, etc. The pitches between c^2 and c^3 are designated d^2, e^2, etc. The same process holds for the pitches below c^1. The pitches between c and c^1 are designated d, e, etc. Those between C and c are designated D, E, etc. And those between CC and C are designated DD, EE, etc.

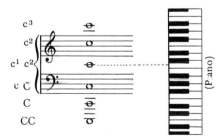

EXERCISE 3-2

Starting with tone c^1, write each pitch on the great staff (ascending and descending) with its name on the next page.

Thus far, only seven of the twelve pitches have been accounted for (C, D, E, F, G, A, B). What about the other five?

Each of the seven pitches C–B can be *raised* by placing a sharp (♯) after it (C + ♯ = C♯) or *lowered* by placing a flat (♭) after it (C + ♭ = C♭).

EXERCISE 3-3

    A Using sharps, fill in the missing pitches between c′ and c³.
    B Using flats, fill in the missing pitches between c′ and C.
    C Play A and B on the piano.

RESULTS

Many of the sharps (♯) and flats (♭) are played on the black keys of the piano. It appears then, that more than twelve pitches can be *notated*, but there are only twelve different *sounding* pitches that we use. The notation of a pitch (C♯ or D♭ depends on its place in a melodic or harmonic context.

C. Tone: Pitch and Quality

Each tone has both specific *pitch* and *quality*. The same tone played on different instruments will have the same pitch but can sound quite differently.

In Exercises 3-4 and 3-5, single tones will be played or sung by different instruments or voices with varied dynamics. Listen to the sound of each example to determine the effect of instrumentation and dynamics on the *quality* of the tone.

EXERCISE 3-4

    A Sing or play c′ on various instruments.
    B Repeat A, varying the dynamics.
    C Double the c′ with various instruments and vary the dynamics.

QUESTIONS AND
OBSERVATIONS

    1 Describe the pitch c′ in Exercise 3-4. Was it always the same c′?
    2 What were the effects of doubling the c′?
    3 What were the effects of altering the dynamics?

Each c′ played or sung had the same frequency, but each had a different sound, depending on its instrumentation and dynamics. In each case, the *quality* of c′ was different.

In addition to doubling and dynamics, the quality of the tone was affected by the nature of the voice or instrument (its construction and material), and the way it produced its sound. Each instrument or voice produces a sound in a particular manner—by being struck, bowed, blown, or sung.

D. Tone Quality: The Overtone Series

With the attack, a *tone* is produced along with "additional" tones called *overtones*. The number and strength of the overtones depends upon the strength and duration of the initial attack and the acoustical properties of the instrument. Overtones are actually a part of the tone, and they give the tone its particular quality. *Tone* is therefore the result of both *pitch* and *quality*.

Overtones, also called *harmonics* or *upper partials*, all relate to the *fundamental tone* as whole-number multiples of the fundamental.

EXERCISE 3-5

Using different dynamics, play C two octaves below c′ on a piano or cello.

QUESTIONS AND
OBSERVATIONS

1 Was the C always the same?

2 Describe what you heard.

3 Describe what you saw as the string was activated.

The entire string C vibrates approximately 65.5 times per second. It also divides itself into two, three, four, and more equal parts, each vibrating as an overtone in a ratio to the fundamental tone—2:1, 3:1, 4:1, and so on. The frequency of these overtones are therefore two times greater (131 cps), three times greater (196.5 cps), four times greater (262 cps), and so on, than the frequency of the fundamental tone. If you could actually *hear* and *see* each overtone and string division, all the tones in the following overtone series would be present in the cello tone C.

names: C   c   G   c¹   e¹   g¹   b♭¹   c²   d²   e²   f♯²   g²   a♭²   b♭²   b♮²   c³

frequency(cps):   65.5   131   195.5   262   327.5   393   458.5   524   589   655   720.5   786   851.5   917   982.5   1048
order of partials: 1   2   3   4   5   6   7   8   9   10   11   12   13   14   15   16

The *quality* of the tone C (or any tone) is determined by the *number, intensity,* and *distribution* of the overtones that are combined (whether they are heard or not) with the fundamental.

The attack activates the vibrations (of a percussion instrument, string, woodwind or brass instrument, or voice) that produce the sound (the tone and its overtones) and the effect of the sound acting on itself. The sound then decays either slowly or quickly, depending on the intensity of the attack and the nature of the instrument. With this sound decay, the quality of the sound changes. This occurs because the *overtone envelope* (the composite grouping of partials) changes as the number, distribution, and strength of the overtones change.

Another important factor of a sound's quality is the listener's position in relation to the sound source. Sitting in different locations in a class or concert hall, you will probably hear the same sound differently. Because sound quality varies with the location of the sound source, the physical placement of instruments and voices should be considered when composing and performing music.

To Sum Up

1 A pitched sound is a tone having a regular wave-form that vibrates periodically a specific number of times per second (cycles per second) to produce a specific frequency.

2 A nonpitched sound is a combination of many wave-forms, each recurring a specific number of times per second. These produce multi-frequencies, which are too confused to be identified as a specific tone. Such frequencies are labeled *noise*. A nonpitched sound combining the entire range of audible frequencies is called *white noise*. This type of sound is very useful in electronic music.

3 The choice and number of instruments and/or voices, and their dynamics, affects the quality of a tone. A sound, therefore, cannot be separated from the instrument or voice that produces it.

4 For the composer, all types of sound, no matter how they are produced, are possible musical materials. All types of sound can be worked with in time and space to produce a musical composition.

PROJECT 3-1

Using graph paper and music paper (pasted onto the graph paper), write a short piece (15 to 30 seconds) that includes:

1 short percussion sounds (hit, tapped, clapped or rubbed sounds, tongue clicks, etc.) made by percussionlike instruments or vocal sounds.

2 sustained vocal and/or instrumental tones.

3 silence, to vary the instrumental-vocal texture.

Consider and notate duration and dynamics carefully. Also consider the texture of the piece carefully as the music moves and changes through time. You should be aware that you are creating a shape-form and working with the complementary musical elements of pitched and non-pitched sounds of various lengths, forms of attack and decay, and dynamics.

LISTENING
SUGGESTIONS

Penderecki: *Threnody* for strings
Crumb: *Ancient Voices of Children*
J. S. Bach: Partita in D minor for solo violin I
Haydn: *Symphony No. 4,* II

Describe each composer's use of sounds (pitched and nonpitched) and silence and the instruments that produce them. Look at at least one of the scores in each group. Observe the way the sounds are notated.

E. Musical Motion: The Succession of Tones

Music, if it were limited to a single sound, could be dull. Dynamics, tempo, and instrumentation help liven up a sound, but new sounds are needed to extend music in time. *Musical motion* is generated by a sound moving to other sounds in succession. A short but coherent melody with just a few tones can generate a sense of musical motion.

Tones can move in two ways and in two directions:

1 *By step,* up   or down

2 By *skip,* to a variety of tones, up or down

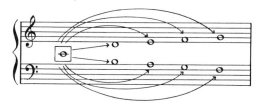

A tone can also be repeated, remaining stationary.

EXERCISE 3-6

Play or sing Examples 3-1–3-4.

Example 3-1. **J. S. Bach:** *"O Ewigkeit, du Donnerwort,"* (two excerpts)

Example 3-2. **J. S. Bach:** *"O Herre Gott, dein Göttlichwort"*

Example 3-3. **Billings:** *"Chester,"* (two excerpts)

Example 3-4. *"Sweet Betsy From Pike"*

QUESTIONS AND OBSERVATIONS

Note the direction of the tones in each of the melodic fragments in Examples 3-1–3-4, and the type of motion (step or skip) used in each.

1 How many successive steps in one direction are there before a tone *skips* to another tone?
2 How many successive skips in one direction are there before a tone moves by step to the next tone?
3 In what direction does the melody move after successive steps or successive skips in one direction?
4 How many times is a specific tone repeated in a melody before it moves to another tone?
5 Do your answers reveal any general patterns?
6 What is the range of each melody?

Each of the melodies in Examples 3-1–3-4 moves up or down, combining steps and skips and at times remaining stationary. Each melody thereby forms a *shape* or *contour*. These contours are as follows:

Example 3-1a. Up:

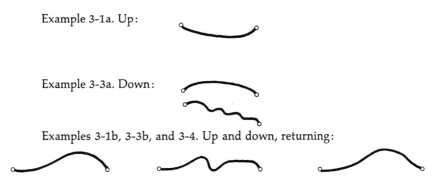

Example 3-3a. Down:

Examples 3-1b, 3-3b, and 3-4. Up and down, returning:

Example 3-2. Down and up, returning and going beyond:

Combinations of various contours exist in more extended melodies.

The range of each melody lies within the eight tones of a diatonic scale.

EXERCISE 3-7

A   Write three short melodies, each with five to eight different tones. Follow these three general contours:

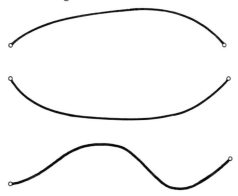

Begin and end each melody with the same tone. Combine steps and skips: balance each skip with step-wise motion in the opposite direction. Repeat tones if you wish.

B   Play or sing each melody.

EXERCISE 3-8

Using other contours, write three additional melodies. Use as many tones as you need. You may finish each melody on the same tone with which you began, or on a different tone.

QUESTIONS AND
OBSERVATIONS

1   Do your melodies hold together?
2   Do they seem complete, or do they need to be extended?
3   Have you balanced your skips with step-wise motion?
4   Suggest ways to improve and/or extend your melodies.
5   Revise them accordingly.

The way you put tones together and the motion that results contribute to the shape-form as it evolves. To be successful, each piece, or part of a piece, depends upon the order and coherence of its parts, which will be perceived as a whole.

PROJECT 3-2

Use Exercise 3-7 or 3-8 as the basis for a short composition (ten to fifteen seconds) for a soprano instrument (such as violin or flute). If you wish, add a percussion part (derived from any exercise in Chapters 1 and 2) that complements the sounds of the soprano instrument.

PROJECT 3-3

Write a short free composition (15 to 30 seconds), using graph paper *and* music paper as needed for the notation of pitch. (Paste or scotch-tape sections of music paper onto the graph paper.) Use whatever musical materials you want from the exercises in Chapters 1–3. A particular exercise that suggests possibilities for elaboration and development could be your starting point.

LISTENING
SUGGESTIONS

Ligeti: *Aventures*
Yannatos: *Cycles II, III*

Observe the various kinds and qualities of vocal and instrumental sounds, pitched and nonpitched.

Berio: *Difference*
Davidovsky: *Synchronisms No. 6*

Observe the complementary use of instrumental and electronic sounds, and the range and quality of these sounds.

J. S. Bach: *Brandenberg Concerto No. 2*

Observe the variation in texture produced by the alteration of solo and tutti (group) sections and the dynamics of the solo and tutti instrumental forces.

BIBLIOGRAPHY: SECTION I

Benade, Arthur H., *Horns, Strings and Harmony*. New York: Doubleday, 1960.

Cage, John, *Silence*. Cambridge, Mass.: M.I.T. Press, 1969.

Hindemith, Paul, *Craft of Musical Composition*, Book I. New York: Associated Music Publishers, 1945.

Sachs, Curt, *The History of Musical Instruments*. New York: Norton, 1953.

Van Bergeijk, William A., John R. Pierce, and Edward E. David, Jr., *Waves and the Ear*. New York: Doubleday, 1960.

Winckel, Fritz, *Music, Sound and Sensation*. New York: Dover, 1967.

Zuckerkandle, Victor, *Sound and Symbol*. Princeton, N. J.: Princeton University Press, 1969.

2 *Space*

To *develop* and awareness of the *real space* through which music moves and the *musical space* that extends throughout the various registers, low to high.

4 BASIC NOTIONS OF SPACE

OBJECTIVES

1. To *study* the relationship of tones to one another.

2. To *consider* how tones can be combined into intervals and chords.

3. To *examine* the relative consonant and dissonant qualities of intervals and chords.

4. To *see* how the various combinations of tones can be used as musical materials.

CAPSULE DEFINITIONS

Interval	Two tones played simultaneously or consecutively.
Chord	Three or more tones sounded together.
Cluster	Many adjacent tones sounded together.
Texture	Density (thickness or thinness of sound).
Octave	Eight-tone distance between two tones (such as c′ and c²).

The exercises in Chapters 1–3 have explored simple forms of musical motion and texture. Musical motion is linked with the flow of time, whereas musical texture "fills up" space. As a sound spreads, extending "up and down," "high and low," musical space is created.

There are two kinds of space. We live and move through *real space*. Sound also moves through real space—outward, from the sound source to the receiver. There is also *musical space*. When we talk of space in music we usually compare it to real space. We talk of high tones and low tones; we say there are higher and lower registers; we hear one chord as *heavier* than another. Musical space, however, is not like real space; it is actually another kind of space.

We know from experience that we can occupy only one place at a time. We also know that two objects cannot occupy the same place at the same time. If one object crosses the path of another, a crash will occur—whether the objects are atoms or autos.

A sound exists in real space. But does a sound, like an object, occupy one place at a time? What happens when a sound is added to other sounds? Do they combine or do they crash?

Any object must use energy and take a certain amount of time to move from place to place. We have heard sounds that seem to move from place to place—from the source to the receiver—within a room, a concert hall, a stadium. Watching a baseball game, seeing the batter hit the ball, and hearing the sound an instant later tells me that the sound took a certain time to travel from the source, the bat, to the receiver, me. Sound appears to behave like objects in that it takes time to move from "here to there."

Sound, like objects moving through space, does encounter the resistance of bodies, chairs, and walls, but it does not "crash" and stop. No matter what blocks or distorts the sound, and no matter how much or how little sound is "soaked up," sound travels around all the impediments and is still recognizable. Its energy can be deflected and diminished, but not immediately obliterated. What remains of the sound occupies all the remaining air space in the enclosure equally.

EXERCISE 4-1

Play the following examples on the piano, softly then forte.

1 The tone c:

2 The interval $\begin{smallmatrix}g\\c:\end{smallmatrix}$

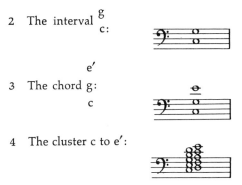

3 The chord $\begin{smallmatrix}e'\\g:\\c\end{smallmatrix}$

4 The cluster c to e′:

QUESTIONS AND
OBSERVATIONS

1 In examples 2 and 3, did you hear each tone as well as all the tones combined?

2 In example 4, did you hear each of the tones in the cluster, or just the tones combined?

The sound of each of these four examples fills the entire room, whether it is played piano or forte. In examples 2–3, each tone as well as the combined sound can be heard. In example 4, it is more difficult to hear each tone, since there are so many of them; all of the tones, however, can be heard as a combined sound with a dense texture.

Music, like an object, takes time to "move." But music also behaves differently than objects do. Objects are *located* in different specific places. Music *moves* in time through the air as sound, equidistantly and simultaneously. Its boundaries are defined only by the total area in which it is sounded—the room, the concert hall, the stadium. Once sounded, music is heard throughout all available space.

Each sound coexists with all other sounds. No one sound replaces another as tone encounters tone, relates, combines, moves out, and occupies all available space equally. Whether a single or a composite sound, its character is not destroyed by real objects (such as bodies and walls) or by musical "objects" (other tones).

One tone or many tones fill up all the available space equally. But we are made more aware of musical space through the impact of texture in the form of the total sound mass and weight of multitone constructions (intervals and chords). We also perceive more depth and weight of sound in real space when the space is "filled up" with many tones that are "higher" or "lower" in relation to one another. It is through texture in the form of these multitone constructions spread throughout a wide range that we perceive a spatial order in music.

EXERCISE 4-2

A Repeat Exercise 4-1, but add the same tone(s) one octave higher.

B   Repeat Exercise 4-1, but add the same tone(s) one octave lower.
C   Repeat Exercise 4-1, but replace the original tone(s) with tone(s) one octave higher and one octave lower.

Real space is needed to make and hear music. A spatial order with "high" and "low" implies a notion of "position," because one tone is heard higher or lower than another. We know that a higher pitch has a higher frequency, and a lower pitch a lower frequency. This is different from saying that one object is higher than another in real space. We already know that one tone, as an "object," cannot replace another tone. Tones coexist. Place does not exist for music in the same way that it does for objects, but a notion of "place" as "position" is still extremely important to the concept of pitch organization.

There is a relationship between one pitch and another in a larger structure—whether that structure is a scale, an interval, or a chord. Each tone in the structure relates to other tones according to its position in the structure, and each functions as a part of an ordered whole. The total structure, which is made up of related tones, intervals, and chords, creates musical space.

We know that tones with specific frequencies relate to one another, and that each occupies musical space. But what about nonpitched sounds? Do they also occupy musical space?

EXERCISE 4-3

A   Repeat Exercise 1-4, but use two contrasting percussion instruments. Play a single nonpitched sound on both instruments simultaneously.
B   Repeat A, joined by your classmates singing two different vocal sounds, such as "sh" and "ss."

RESULTS

In Exercise 4-3, there were different pitch levels of sound, which could be considered part of a "higher" or "lower" register.

Nonpitched sounds relate to each other as high or low, loud or soft, thicker or thinner. Since composers select their musical materials, their choices involve the notion of relationship—that is, position and function. When one tone is related to another tone or to a nonpitched sound, the resulting combination greatly enriches the texture, delineates the position of each sound in relation to the other, and extends the sense of musical space.

To Sum Up

We borrowed concepts of space and place from the real world and applied them by analogy to music. But these concepts have specific meanings of their own as they are applied to music. We move in real space, and music moves in real space. We, as objects, occupy place and encounter resistance in other objects as we move from place to place. As music encounters objects in real space, it fills all the remaining space equally. We can only occupy one space at a time. One tone, many tones, or other sounds coexist and occupy all the space simultaneously.

Place does exist for musical sound. Each tone or sound exists in *relation* to each other tone or sound as defined by its position (high or low, loud or soft, thick or thin) in a scale, an interval, a chord, or a multilevel sound complex. Each sound, through its texture, creates musical space. The more tones or levels of sound, the greater the sense of musical space, weight, and depth of spatial extension.

The evolving concepts of space and musical space have fundamentally affected the development of music. Music has continually moved *outward* into musical space, from the one-part music of Gregorian chant to the multisound complexes of the twentieth century.

These concepts will become clearer as we begin to work with intervals and chords.

LISTENING
SUGGESTIONS

Beethoven: *Symphony No. 5*, transition from third to fourth movements
Debussy: *Nocturnes*: "Nuages"
Brant: *Signs and Alarms*

Listen for each composer's use of tonal register, dynamics, and texture.

PROJECT 4-1

Use single tones and multitone combinations to experiment with "space" in the various registers of the piano. Use extreme dynamics (*fff* , *ppp*) and then silence for dramatic effect and to create a sense of space. You may also introduce nonpitched percussion sounds.

ANALYSIS 4-1

Examine the score while listening to the first movement of Beethoven's Piano Sonata, Op. 53 (*Waldstein*), for its use of different tonal registers, dynamics, and texture. Be prepared to comment on these aspects of the piece.

5 MUSICAL SPACE:
The Interval

OBJECTIVES

1. To *identify* simple and compound intervals.
2. To *create* musical motion and texture in simple two-voice pieces.

CAPSULE DEFINITIONS

Scale	A succession of ascending and descending tones with a fixed interval structure.
Scale forms	Major, minor, chromatic, pentatonic, whole-tone, etc.
Motion	Sense of direction in music of one or more parts.
Types of motion	*parallel:* two or more voices move in the same direction, and at the same distance from one another.
	similar: two or more voices move in the same direction, but not at the same distance from one another.
	oblique: one voice remains stationary while one or more voices move.
	contrary: voices move in opposite directions.
Tempo	Time, rate of movement, or speed.
Step	A whole tone.
Halfstep	A semitone.
Simple interval	Two tones that fall within the range of one octave.

A. Preliminary Explorations

The first extension into musical space beyond the single tone is the interval. Any two tones sounded *together* as one sound event 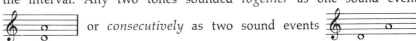 or *consecutively* as two sound events make up an interval. The interval has both harmonic and melodic possibilities.

When two melodic voices or parts are played together, each of the two tones combines *harmonically* into an interval. When one tone moves to another tone, an interval occurs *melodically*. An interval moves to other intervals whether formed harmonically or melodically.

EXERCISE 5-1

A Play or sing with one or more of your classmates:

B Does each interval formed harmonically sound the same? (Describe the sound.)
C Describe the movement from interval to interval.
D Describe the movement from tone to tone (by step or skip, up or down) in the top voice; in the bottom voice.

EXERCISE 5-2

A Play or sing:

B Does each interval formed melodically sound the same? (Describe the sound.)
C Describe the movement from tone to tone (by step or skip, up or down).
D Outline the contour of the melody.

RESULTS

Many different intervals can be formed, each with its own special sound. The placement of the interval in musical space also affects its sound:

The *size* of an interval is the distance between its two tones. One way of measuring an interval's size is to determine the ratio of the frequencies of the two tones. (See the discussion of the overtone series in Chapter 3).

EXERCISE 5-3

C' has a frequency of 262 cps, c^2 a frequency of 524 cps, and g' a frequency of 393 cps.

A   What is the ratio of the frequencies of c' and c^2?

B   What is the ratio of the frequencies of c' and g'?

RESULTS   In Exercise 5-3 A and B, the ratio of the frequency is 2:1 and 3:2. Musicians usually refer to the intervals in Exercise 5-3 as *octaves* and *fifths* rather than as ratios of 2 to 1 and 3 to 2, respectively.

In Exercises 5-4 and 5-5, the tones of a C major scale (Example 5-1) will be used to determine the general size of each interval (fifth, fourth, etc.). Each tone in the scale (from c' to c^2) is numbered from *1* to *8*. Using c' as tone *1*, we can calculate the size of an interval by measuring the distance between c' and any other tone in the scale. For example, the distance between c' and d' is from tone *1* to tone *2*, or a *second*.

Example 5-1.   The tones of a C major scale

EXERCISE 5-4

Play or sing each of the following intervals. Using the C major scale (Example 5-1), with c′ as the bottom tone (*1*), calculate the size of each interval.

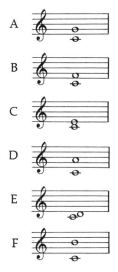

Any tone can serve as a *bottom* or *bass* tone of an interval. Any bottom tone would then be called *1*. For example, if g′, which was *5* in Example 5-1, became the new *1*, the distance between g′ and c² would be *1* to *4*, or a fourth.

EXERCISE 5-5

Play or sing with one or more of your classmates each of the following intervals. Then calculate the size of each interval.

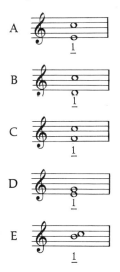

F
1

In Exercises 5-4 and 5-5, the general size of various intervals was measured. To measure the *specific* size of an interval in order to determine the *kind* of interval (major, minor, etc.), we need to know the precise number of *half steps* and *whole steps* each interval contains. For this, we will use a chromatic scale (with the piano keyboard represented) of twelve half steps or *semitones*, numbered *0* to *12* from c′ to c². (see Example 5-2). For example, c′ to d′ is one whole step (a major second) that consists of two half steps. Each half step is a minor second or its equivalent (c′ to c♯ or d♭′, c♯ or d♭′ to d′).

Example 5-2.   Chromatic scale and keyboard

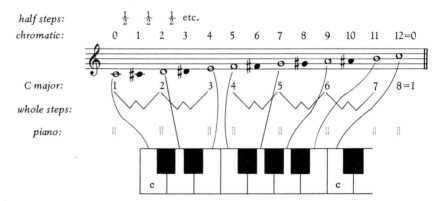

EXERCISE 5-6

With c′ as the bass, calculate the number of half steps (top of Example 5-2) and then the number of whole and half steps (bottom of Example 5-2) in each of the intervals in Exercise 5-4 and in each of the six intervals presented below. List them.

For example, 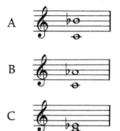 = *0* to *12* = twelve half steps or five whole steps and two half steps = an octave (8^{ve}).

A

B

C

EXERCISE 5-6
(VARIATION)

Count the number of half steps and then the number of whole and half steps in each of the intervals in Exercise 5-5. (Use the bottom tone of each interval as *1*.) List them.

B. Simple Intervals: Perfect, Major, and Minor

All the intervals in Exercises 5-1 through 5-6 are called *simple* intervals because each occurs within the space of one octave. The *octave*, *fifth*, and *fourth* can be perfect (P), augmented (A), or diminished (d).

EXERCISE 5-7

A Sing or play with one or more of your classmates the perfect intervals in Exercises 5–4 and 5–5.

B How many half steps and how many whole and half steps does each interval contain? List them.

C Describe the character of each of the six intervals and the differences in character among them.

The *second, third, sixth,* and *seventh* can be major, minor, augmented, or diminished.

EXERCISE 5-8

A Sing or play with one or more of your classmates the major intervals and then the minor intervals in Exercises 5–4 and 5–5.

B What is the difference between a major and a minor interval: in size? in character? What determines the difference?

C Describe the character of each interval and the differences in character among them.

D Compare the general character of the intervals in Exercise 5–7 with that of the intervals in Exercise 5–8. Is there a basic difference?

EXERCISE 5-9

Play, sing, or write Example 5-3:

A in unison

B in perfect octaves (up, down, up and down).

C in perfect fifths (up, down).

D in perfect fourths (up, down).

E in perfect fifths (up) and perfect fourths (down).

F in perfect fourths (up) and perfect fifths (down).

G in major thirds (up, down).

H in minor thirds (up, down).

I in major sixths (up, down).

J in minor sixths (up, down).

K in major seconds (up, down).

L in minor seconds (up, down).

M in major sevenths (up, down).

N in minor sevenths (up, down).

Example 5-3.   Melody based on the *"Dies Irae,"* (13th century plainsong)

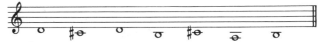

QUESTIONS AND
OBSERVATIONS

1 Do the various two-part textures A–N sound the same? Describe.

2 Do some intervals sound more tense and dissonant than others?

3 Would you mention the "tenseness" of an interval in describing its character? Its quality?

4 Do intervals moving in the same direction at the same distance (parallel motion), as in Exercise 5-9, sound interesting?

5 Suggest ways to harmonize the "Dies Irae" melody so that the intervals are not always equidistant.

Example 5-4.   Pentatonic melody harmonized

EXERCISE 5-10

    A Add another part, above or below, to Example 5-3. Use a variety of intervals in the added part.

    B Play or sing with one or more of your classmates the resulting composition.

    C Describe what you tried to do.

    D Does it work?

EXERCISE 5-11

    A Play or sing with one or more of your classmates the upper part of Example 5-4, which is based on a pentatonic scale in unison.

    B Play or sing both parts of Example 5-4.

QUESTIONS AND   1 Describe the harmonic and melodic movement of both parts.

OBSERVATIONS   2 Is there a point in the piece that sounds most tense? Why?

C. Musical Motion—Two Part Texture

One or more parts that mimic each other, moving in the same direction with a fixed interval, create little tension over a period of time. Composers have used this type of parallel musical motion to good effect in Gregorian chant and in rock progressions.

To create a greater sense of musical motion and variety of texture, we can construct a second part in several ways:

    1 A second part can move in a direction *similar* to that of the melody, with changing intervals:

    2 It can proceed in *oblique* motion: repeating a tone while the melody changes:

    3 It can move in *contrary* motion: each of the two parts moves in opposite directions:

The several types of musical motion can be combined in a variety of ways in the course of a piece.

In the following three exercises, the four types of musical motion will be created by the use of nonpitched vocal sounds and then by the use of tones.

EXERCISE 5-12

You and your classmates should divide into two groups. Group I sings the vocal sound "sh"; Group II sings the vocal sound "ss."

A   Make a cresc. () and then a dim. ( ) together:

B   Group I makes its cresc. ( ) *slightly* faster than Group II; begin the dim. ( ) together, but I makes its dim. ( ) slightly faster:

C   I sustains its sound while II makes a cresc.; I then makes its cresc. along with II:

D   I makes a cresc. and then a dim., while II makes a dim. and then a cresc.:

E   Repeat A–D with one voice on a part.

QUESTIONS AND
OBSERVATIONS

1   Did you hear two distinct parts?
2   Describe the effects of the cresc. and dim. on the *general* pitch of the vocal sounds.
3   Did you have a sense of the various types of musical motion you created? Describe.
4   What was the effect on the texture of doubling the vocal sounds with many voices. Was the effect the same with one voice on a part? Describe the differences.

EXERCISES
5-9 and 5-11
(VARIATIONS)

Repeat, using:

1   different dynamics.
2   different vocal or instrumental forces.
3   different durations.
4   different speeds.

EXERCISE 5-13

A   Transpose the melody of Example 5-4 down one octave into the bass clef. Write a second part above it, using parallel, similar, oblique, and contrary motion.

B   Describe the harmonic and melodic movement in each case, indicating the intervals formed by the tones sounding together and the intervals formed by the movement from tone to tone in each of the two parts.

To Sum Up   Each tone, interval, or nonpitched sound moving in various directions can create different textures as well as musical motion.

D. Simple Intervals: Augmented and Diminished

Every interval can be *altered*. We can *enlarge* any interval a semitone (half step), either by raising the top tone or lowering the bottom tone. We can also *reduce* any interval a semitone, by lowering the top tone or raising the bottom tone.

EXERCISE 5-14

A   Take each of the minor intervals in Exercises 5-5 and 5-6 and enlarge it a semitone (raise the top or lower the bass).

B   Play or sing each altered interval.

C   Describe the result of enlarging a minor interval by a semitone.

EXERCISE 5-15

A   Take each of the major intervals in Exercise 5-4 and reduce it a semitone.

B   Play or sing each altered interval.

C   Describe the result of lowering a major interval a semitone.

EXERCISE 5-16

A   Enlarge all perfect fourths in Exercises 5-4 and 5-5 a semitone.

B   Reduce all perfect fifths in Exercises 5-4 and 5-5 a semitone.

C   Play or sing each interval.

D   Compare these intervals in A and B with those in Exercise 5-6, E and F.

E   Describe the difference between the sound of a perfect fourth and a fourth that has been enlarged a semitone; between a perfect fifth and a fifth that has been reduced a semitone.

EXERCISES
5-14–5-16
(VARIATIONS)

A   Enlarge each major interval a semitone.

B   Reduce each minor interval a semitone.

C   Enlarge each perfect interval a semitone; reduce each a semitone.

D   Play or sing each of the intervals in A, B, and C.

E   Do some intervals sound like other intervals even though they are written differently? Which intervals?

F   Write each of these intervals so that they look as they sound.

RESULTS   1. A minor interval enlarged a semitone becomes a major interval; reduced a semitone, it becomes a *diminished* interval.

2. A major interval reduced a semitone becomes a minor interval; enlarged a semitone, it becomes an *augmented* interval.

3. A perfect interval enlarged a semitone becomes an augmented interval; reduced a semitone, it becomes a diminished interval.

4. Intervals that sound alike even though they are written differently contain the same number of semitones.

ADDITIONAL
EXERCISES

1. Take intervals that sound alike but are written differently. Calculate the number of semitones in each.

2. Review Exercises 5-14–5-16.

A. Play or sing each interval in these exercises until you can easily recognize it.

B. On the piano or another instrument, transpose each interval one and then two octaves up and down, so that you distinguish it in different registers.

C. Transpose each interval to different pitches.

PROJECT 5-1

Experiment with a series of simple intervals. (Use augmented and diminished intervals sparingly.) Write the intervals in the middle register (c'). Then transpose them to different registers of the piano (or to two instruments). Use dynamics, duration, and register to create a varied, two-voice-textured piece with a sense of musical flow.

PROJECT 5-2

Take a melody (for example, "Dies Irae") and extend it by repetition, transposition, and augmentation (lengthening the duration of the melody tones). Harmonize the melody with various intervals and types of motion in order to create an interesting texture.

LISTENING
SUGGESTIONS

J. S. Bach: Invention No. 1
Schoenberg: *Six Little Piano Pieces*, Op. 19, No. 2

Note the intervals and the types of intervallic motion in each piece, and the style of each piece.

ANALYSIS 5-1

Examine Example 5-5.

A   Play each part slowly on the piano.
B   Combine both parts.
C   Mark each interval below the bottom part.
D   Describe the motion of the two parts, and the texture it creates.

Example 5-5.   **J. S. Bach:** *Little Notebook for Anna Magdalena Bach, aria*

ANALYSIS 5-2

Examine Example 5-6.

A   Play each part individually.
B   Play the upper parts together.
C   Play the lower parts together, listening to each interval.
D   In each excerpt, mark all of the intervals: mark the intervals in the bottom line (𝄢) below the bottom line; mark the intervals in the top line (𝄞) above the top line.

Example 5-6.   **Bartók:** *MikroKosmos,* Vol. III, No. 71 and 83 (two excerpts)

6 THE INTERVAL: Musical Context

OBJECTIVES

1. To *recognize* the tonal tendencies of intervals.
2. To *connect* and resolve intervals in simple two-voice pieces.

CAPSULE DEFINITIONS

Tonal tendency	The gravitation of one tone to another.
Spelling	The way tones are written.
Voice (or part)	In multipart music, soprano, alto, tenor, and bass.
Compound interval	Two tones whose interval is larger than an octave.
Stable intervals	Generally considered to be consonant intervals.
Unstable intervals	Generally considered to be less consonant intervals that ordinarily move or resolve to more consonant intervals.
Inversion	Transposition of the lower tone of an interval above the top tone; transposition of the upper tone of an interval below the bottom tone.
Phrase	A cohesive musical idea or portion of a melody.
Twelve-tone row	A melodic and/or harmonic arrangement of the twelve tones of the chromatic scale.
Different forms of the twelve-tone row	*original (O):* The original melodic and/or harmonic arrangement of the twelve tones of the chromatic scale. *inversion (I):* upside down. *retrograde (R):* backward. *retrograde inversion (RI):* backward and upside down.

A. Simple Intervals: Tonal Tendencies

Why do composers sometimes use complicated spellings of intervals when they could write them simply?

An interval moves to other intervals and creates musical motion. Each tone of an interval also moves to a tone of another interval. The spelling of each tone of the interval can indicate its movement to the tone of the next interval. If a tone is a part of an ascending or descending line, its spelling is important as a means of indicating the direction of its movement or resolution.

Examples 6-1 and 6-2 contain augmented and diminished intervals. Ordinarily, these intervals are treated as *unstable intervals*—that is, intervals that tend to move or resolve up or down to more stable intervals.

Example 6-1.   **Beethoven:** *Piano Sonata*, Op. 2, No. 1, minuet, m. 22

Example 6-2.   **Wagner:** *Tristan and Isolde:* "Prelude and Love Death," mm. 2–3

In one sense, only the unison and octave are fully stable intervals. The other intervals contain some degree of tension or dissonance that can move or resolve to more stable intervals.

EXERCISE 6-1

A   Play each interval in groups I–III.

B   Which group contains intervals that sound consonant and stable? The least consonant and the most unstable?

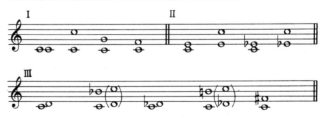

54

In Exercises 6-2 and 6-3, various intervals move or resolve to other intervals. Observe their movement, their sound, and their *position* in the musical phrase.

EXERCISE 6-2

A   Mark the intervals in Example 6-3 below the example.

Example 6-3.   Two excerpts from *Clausulae for "Hec Dies,"* (thirteenth century, style of Perotin)

B   Mark the intervals in each chord in Example 6-4: mark the intervals in the soprano and alto parts (𝄞) above the example, the tenor and bass parts (𝄢) below the example, and the alto and tenor parts (𝄞𝄢) in between.

Example 6-4.   Two excerpts from **J. S. Bach:** *"Herzlich tut mich Verlangen"*

QUESTIONS AND
OBSERVATIONS

1   How does each interval in Examples 6-3 and 6-4 move or resolve?
2   Why are tones spelled the way they are in Example 6-4?
3   From what part of the phrase is each example taken?

In Examples 6-3 and 6-4, the tendency of less stable intervals to move or resolve to more stable intervals was present in their *sound*, their *function*, and their *position* in the phrase. The intervals in group I of Exercise 6-1 are the most consonant and stable, those in group II fairly consonant and stable, and those in group III the most dissonant and unstable.

Ordinarily, consonant intervals begin and end a phrase. In Example

6-3a, this occurs at the beginning of the phrase: 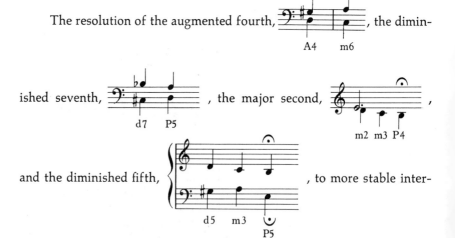 and at

the end: . In Example 6-3b, it occurs at the end of

the phrase: . (The perfect fourth, though con-

sonant, is considered somewhat unstable in tonal music; it usually resolves to a third.)

The resolution of the augmented fourth, , the dimin-

ished seventh, , the major second, ,

and the diminished fifth, , to more stable inter-

vals occurs at the beginning of the phrase (Example 6-4a) and at the end of the phrase (Example 6-4b). The tension these unstable intervals create gives the phrase a "push" at its beginning and a feeling of resolution at its conclusion. Observe in Example 6-4 that raised tones (marked by a ♯) move upward and lowered tones (marked by a ♭) move downward.

EXERCISE 6-3

A. Complete each of the following examples, resolving each interval by stepwise motion, up or down. In each case, add tones that will give the example a feeling of resolution.

B. Play or sing each example.
C. Describe the type of motion used in each example.
D. Correct your results.

RESULTS   The *actual sound* of each interval, with its inherent degree of stability and tension, and the *musical situation* limited the motion of tones and the resolution of intervals. Unstable intervals tend to move or resolve in certain ways. However, a composer can delay or impede a normal resolution of such an interval for musical purposes.

EXERCISE 6-3
(VARIATIONS)

A   Delay each resolution in Exercise 6-3 by inserting additional tones in one part.
B   Play or sing the new version.

B. Simple Intervals: Inversion and Transposition

Any interval can be transposed to any register:  .

Any one tone of an interval can be transposed to any register:

If the lower tone of any interval is transposed above the upper tone:

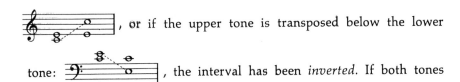 , or if the upper tone is transposed below the lower

tone: , the interval has been *inverted*. If both tones

remain within the octave after transposition, the interval remains a *simple interval*. An interval that is inverted has changed its size.

In Exercises 6-4 through 6-6, simple intervals will be inverted. Name each new interval, and observe its relationship to the original interval.

EXERCISE 6-4

A   Transpose the bass of Exercise 5-4 up one octave. For example:

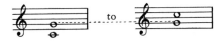

B   Transpose the soprano of Exercise 5-4 down one octave. For example:

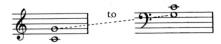

EXERCISE 6-5

A   Transpose the bass of Exercise 5-1 up one octave.
B   Transpose the soprano of Exercise 5-1 down one octave.

RESULTS

1   A major interval inverts to a minor interval, and vice versa.
2   A perfect interval inverts to a perfect interval.
3   Seconds invert to sevenths, thirds to sixths, and fourths to fifths.

What do augmented and diminished intervals invert to? Are the inversions as stable or as unstable as their originals?

EXERCISE 6-6

Invert each interval in Exercise 6-3:

A   Transpose the bass up one octave. For example:

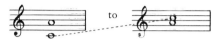

B   Transpose the soprano down one octave. For example:

Do the interval resolutions sound convincing in their inverted form? Write other possible resolutions, adding accidentals or changing one tone of the interval.

PROJECT 6-1

Rewrite Project 5-1 or 5-2, inverting some of the intervals. Does the piece sound the same? Describe.

PROJECT 6-2

A   Using both stable and less stable intervals, write a bass line to the twelve-tone row in Example 6-5.
B   Invert the parts.
C   Harmonize the twelve-tone row in retrograde form (backwards) and an octave lower—or on another pitch level. For a better control of interval resolutions, move more freely rhythmically, holding a tone while the other tone of the interval moves.

Example 6-5.   **Dallapiccola:** Twelve-tone row from *Quaderno Musicale di Annalibera*

ANALYSIS 6-1

Choose any four pieces from the popular, folk, and classical repetoires.

A   Describe the basic intervals used.

B   Describe the types of motion of the melody in relation to a moving part(s).

C. Compound Intervals

In addition to simple intervals, there are intervals larger than an octave. In Examples 6-6 and 6-7 each interval is larger than an octave. All intervals larger than an octave are called *compound intervals*.

Example 6-6.   **Hopkinson:** *"My Days Have Been So Wondrous Free"*

Example 6-7.   **Mozart:** *Piano Sonata, K. 331*

In Exercises 6-7 and 6-8, one tone of a simple interval will be transposed so that the interval becomes a compound interval. Name each new interval, and observe its relationship to the original interval.

EXERCISE 6-7

Transpose the soprano of Exercise 5-4 up one octave. For example:

EXERCISE 6-8

Transpose the bass of Exercise 5-5 down one octave. For example:

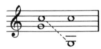

ADDITIONAL
EXERCISES

1   Rewrite Exercises 5-9 and 5-10 so that the simple intervals are made
    into compound intervals. Play the original version. Play the new
    version.

2   Rewrite Exercise 6-3 so that the simple intervals are made into com-
    pound intervals. Do the interval resolutions *still* sound convincing?
    Write other possible resolutions.

To Sum Up

1. Every interval can be transposed up or down.

2. Any note of an interval can be transposed up or down.

3. Every interval can therefore be inverted (or turned upside down
—from a fourth to a fifth, a third to a sixth, a second to a seventh, etc.).

4. Register (place), instrumentation, and size affect an interval's
quality and its degree of "harshness" or *dissonance*.

PROJECT 6-3

Use any exercise or project in Chapters 5 and 6 as the basis for a
short composition for piano and/or voices, or for piano and/or other
instruments (percussion optional). The tones of an interval *need not*
always be sounded together—one tone can be held as the other changes.

Sharps, flats, and slides (*glissandi* or "smearing") from tone to
tone can be used, as well as variations in the tone's duration, register, and
dynamics. Single tones or whole intervals can be *doubled* (more than
one instrument or voice on the same note, or on a note one or two octaves
apart, and so on) for dramatic effect and greater physical sense of weight
(mass) and extended musical space.

PROJECT 6-4

Use Project 6-2 as the basis for an enlarged piece that incorporates
simple and compound intervals. To extend the twelve-tone melody, you
can repeat, transpose, or invert it. For the second part, you can use the
retrograde (backward), the original or retrograde in inverted form at the
same pitch level, or transposed up or down to a different pitch level.

LISTENING
SUGGESTIONS

Stravinsky: *Symphony of Psalms*, first movement

Observe the use of intervals as opposed to chords.

Dallapiccola: *Quaderno Musicale di Annalibera*, No. 5

Observe the juxtaposition of compound and simple intervals.

Brahms: *Symphony No. 3*, first movement

Observe the use of register—high, low, and middle.

ANALYSIS 6-2

A   Examine and then play Example 6-8, a composition by six-year-old Wolfgang Mozart.
B   Write the name of each interval.
C   Invert the two parts. Is it the same piece?

Example 6-8.   **Mozart:** *Minuet*

ANALYSIS 6-3

A   Examine and then play Example 6-9.
B   Write the name of each interval.

Example 6-9.   *"Mira Lege, Miro Modo"* (twelfth century, two-part organum)

7 THE INTERVAL:
Consonance and Dissonance

OBJECTIVES

1. To *learn* to hear the relative consonant and dissonant quality of intervals.

2. To *recognize* the roots of intervals and their relationship to each other.

3. To *use* both aspects of intervals to write simple two-voice pieces.

CAPSULE DEFINITIONS

Root	Dominating tone of an interval or chord.
Consonance; dissonance	Relative degree of "tension" of sounds.
Combination (or resultant) tones	"Extra" tones that result when two or more tones are sounded together.
Cadence	Harmonic and/or melodic "breathing" point at the end of a phrase.

A. Preliminary Explorations

The concept of consonance and dissonance in Western music has always been controversial. What is considered dissonant at one time is later accepted as consonant. New "dissonant" intervals have always been accepted after some initial resistance.

"New" intervals—the fifth and the fourth—were first used "harmonically" in the Middle Ages when a second part was added to the Gregorian chant. Later, with the development of music of three or more parts, "newer harmonic intervals" were used—thirds, sixths, sevenths, and the tritone (an augmented fourth or diminished fifth), which was called the "devil in music" (*Diabolus in Musica*).

Today, our complex musical language includes *multitone sounds*, such as tone clusters and multichords; *nonpitched sounds*, such as tape and electronic sounds and multifrequency sounds called "white noise," and various pitched and nonpitched vocal and instrumental "effects." To label any sound "consonant" or "dissonant" today is very difficult, for today's composer can use all sounds to musical ends. However, we do need to study consonance and dissonance so that we can draw our own conclusions as to how dissonant a sound is relative to other sounds, and how both consonant and dissonant sounds can be used musically.

Consonance and dissonance have always constituted a set of "poles" in Western music. If these are felt simply as "more" or "less" tension or dissonance, then the idea of consonance and dissonance has meaning in music. This is so even though there is no completely adequate explanation of dissonance; that is, no explanation of dissonance accounts for *all* the various elements present in a single musical moment.

As a first step, in Exercise 6-1, we grouped intervals in three general categories, ranging from the most stable and consonant (group I) to the least stable and consonant (group III).

In Exercises 7-1 through 7-5, the overtone series will be used to explore the consonant/dissonant character of intervals in greater detail.

EXERCISE 7-1

A   Construct an overtone series from c to c^3.
B   Reduce the series to a chord.
C   Construct an overtone series from g to d^3.
D   Reduce the series to a chord.
E   Play the fundamentals of A and C together as an interval of a

perfect fifth:

F Examine the harmonics of c and g. Note those partials that are common to both tones and those that are not.

EXERCISE 7-2

A Construct an overtone series from d to d^3.
B Reduce the series to a chord.
C Play the fundamentals of A and Exercise 7-1C together as an interval of a perfect fourth:

D Examine the harmonics of d and g. Note those partials that are common to both tones and those that are not.

EXERCISE 7-3

A Write the reduced versions (i.e., chords) of Exercises 7-1B and 7-2B, and compare.
B Play the fundamentals of A (c and d) together as an interval of a major second:

C Examine the harmonics of c and d. Note those partials that are common to both tones and those that are not.

RESULTS

The perfect fifth c and g ( ) will produce common

partials (g', g^2). The perfect fourth d and g ( ) will do the same (d^2, d^3).

The major second c and d will produce no common partials. The frequency ratio of the perfect fifth is 3:2, that of the perfect fourth is 4:3, and that of the major second is 9:8. Hermann von Helmholtz, in his theory of the relation of sounds, defines consonance as two tones having one or more tones in common. The fifth and the fourth have two tones in common; the second has none. (Helmholtz doesn't include the "higher" partials, which have less effect on the sound.)

How many common tones in a:

1   major third?

2   minor third?

3   minor sixth?

(Use Exercises 7-1 through 7-3 as a guide in arriving at your answers.)

Helmholtz, in his theory of beats, states that two tones sounded together create *beats* of the upper partials. These beats break up the sound mass into pulses of tone, which result in a "rough" effect. Beats, which are the differences in frequency between two tones, are heard as twanging pulses of sound. Slightly "out of tune" piano strings or instruments will blend into a single tone with slight but regular fluctuations of loudness that are actually the peaks in oscillation of the *beat frequency* (the differences in frequency between the nearly equal tones).

In Exercises 7-4 and 7-5, we will measure more accurately the degree of dissonance of the various intervals in Exercises 7-1 through 7-3 by examining those partials that are *not* common to both tones but are close enough to excite beat frequencies. For example, in Exercise 7-1,

$e^2 = 655$ cps
$d^2 = 589$ cps
$c^2 = 524$ cps

The difference between e^2 and d^2 is 66 cps; between d^2 and C^2, 65 cps.

EXERCISE 7-4

(Refer to Exercise 7-2.)

$b^2 = 982.5$ cps $a^2 = 880$ cps

$g^2 = 786$ cps $f\sharp^2 = 720.5$ cps

$g' = 393$ cps $a\ = 440$ cps

What is the difference in frequency between

b^2 and a^2?

g^2 and a^2?

g^2 and $f\sharp^2$?

g' and a'?

EXERCISE 7-5

(Refer to Exercise 7-3.)

$g^2 = 786$ cps $a^2 = 880$ cps

$e^2 = 655$ cps $f\sharp^2 = 720.5$ cps

$c^2 = 524$ cps $d^2 = 589$ cps

$g' = 393$ cps $a' = 440$ cps

$c' = 262$ cps $d' = 294.5$ cps

What is the difference in frequency between

g^2 and a^2?

g^2 and $f\sharp^2$?

e^2 and $f\sharp^2$?

e^2 and d^2?

c^2 and d^2?

g' and a'?

c' and d'?

RESULTS   The fewer common partials in an interval, the greater the number of dissimilar partials that will create beats. The greater the number of beats, the greater the degree of dissonance.

ADDITIONAL
EXERCISES

1   Does a minor second have any common tones in the overtone series?

2   Does a tritone? (Use Exercises 7-1 through 7-3 as a guide.)

3   Does a major seventh?

Group I comprises the most consonant intervals—the perfec octave, perfect fifth, and perfect fourth. These intervals contain two overtones in common:

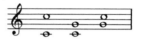

Group II comprises consonant imperfect intervals—the major and minor third and sixth. These intervals contain one overtone in common:

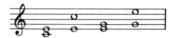

Group III comprises the least consonant intervals—the major and minor second and seventh, the augmented fourth, and the diminished fifth. These intervals contain no overtones in common, except for partials that are so high in the overtone series that they are quite weak:

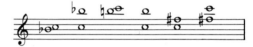

The most harmonically stable intervals (groups I and II) are the most consonant intervals. Harmonic stability decreases with the increasing dissonance of intervals (group II). But we must qualify this. The perfect fourth, and to a lesser degree the major and minor sixth, can *appear* less stable in musical situations than its grouping implies. Intervallic stability, then, also depends on the position of the interval's dominant tone, which serves as its fundamental tone, or *root* (a term more often applied to chords, but applied to intervals by Hindemith). The fifth and third with the root on the bottom is more stable than the fourth and the sixth with the root on the top.

B. Consonance and Dissonance: Other Contributing Factors

Before exploring the roots of intervals, there are other factors to be considered that contribute to the consonant/dissonant character of an interval. These include *placement* and *register*, *dynamics*, the *instrumental quality* and *duration* of an interval, and *tempo* (the rate of movement from interval to interval).

Placement
and
Register   A major second (⨀) is more dissonant than its inversion, a minor seventh (⨀). Widening the space of the major second

to a compound interval of a major ninth (♮:𝄞) will further decrease its dissonant quality.

EXERCISE 7-6

    A Play each interval in Exercises 6-7 and 6-8.

    B Describe the difference in sound between the simple and compound form of each interval.

    C Transpose each compound interval in Exercise 6-7 up one octave; up two octaves. Play each interval.

    D Widen each compound interval in Exercise 6-7, keeping the same bass but transposing the soprano up one octave; up two octaves. Play each interval.

    E Widen each compound interval in Exercise 6-8, keeping the same soprano but transposing the bass down one octave; down two octaves. Play each interval.

    F Which version of each interval in C through E is more dissonant? Which is least dissonant? Why?

In Exercises 7-7 and 7-8, the consonant/dissonant character of intervals will be explored as they are affected by dynamics, instrumentation, duration, and tempo.

C. Dynamics, Instrumentation (Instrumental Quality)

EXERCISE 7-7

Example 7-1.   Music

    A Play or sing with one or more of your classmates Example 7-1 piano (*p*).

    B Play or sing with one or more of your classmates Example 7-1 forte (*f*).

    C Play or sing with one or more of your classmates the soprano part (I) piano and the base part (II) forte.

    D Reverse the dynamics of C.

E

F Reverse the dynamics of E.
G

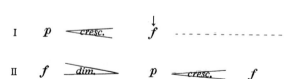

H Reverse the dynamics of G.
I Change the instrumentation of any of the above.

D. Duration, Instrumentation, Tempo

EXERCISE 7-8

Example 7-2.

Sing or play Examples 7-1 and 7-2 as follows:

A

          (staccato)

        I *ḟ* (rest)

          (legato) etc.

       II *p*

B Reverse the dynamics and duration of the two parts in A.
C

        I *ṗ* (rest)

             etc.

       II *f*

D Reverse the dynamics and duration of C.

E

I   *p* (rest)   *f* ⟼ *p* (rest)   *f* ⟼

                                                                  etc.

II   *f* ⟼ *p* (rest)   *f* ⟼ *p* (rest)

F   Reverse the dynamics and duration of E.

G

I   *p* ⟼ *f* (rest)   *p* ⟼ *f* (rest)

                                                                etc.

II   *f* (rest)   *p* ⟼ *f* (rest)   *p* ⟼

H   Reverse the dynamics and duration of G.
I   Change the instrumentation of any of the above.
J   Increase the tempo of any of the above.

QUESTIONS AND OBSERVATIONS

1   Do the consonant intervals (groups I and II, p. 54) always sound consonant? Do the more dissonant intervals (group III), always sound dissonant?

2   What factor(s) affected the quality of the intervals that changed their consonant/dissonant character? How? (Look at specific exercises.)

ADDITIONAL EXERCISES

1   Transpose Exercises 7-7 and 7-8 up or down one or two octaves. Change the instrumentation.

2   Transpose either part of Exercises 7-7, 7-8 up or down one or two octaves. Change the instrumentation.

To Sum Up   Those intervals with more overtones in common *tend* to be more consonant than those with fewer or no overtones in common. Dynamics, register, duration, and instrumentation —factors that influence the quality of a tone—also affect the consonant/dissonant character of an interval.

The rate of change of intervals (*tempo*) also affects the quality of the interval. Instruments must "attack" each sound—whether bowed, blown, or struck—at different speeds, depending upon the tempo. There is a certain amount of sound residue, especially at faster tempos, where one sound overlaps as another is initiated. This residue creates mixes of *combined sounds*, which contribute to the dissonant character of the intervals being played.

Musical context, or the relationship and meaning of sounds in a musical structure, also affects the consonant/dissonant character of intervals. A major third, dramatically interjected into the context of a single line or the context of two parts with perfect intervals, can sound very significant.

Knowing how tones combine into intervals and how they interact with other intervals is essential in controlling the musical flow.

LISTENING
SUGGESTION

Debussy: Nocturnes: "Nuages" and "Fêtes"

Compare the opening passage of "Nuages" and the opening passage of part II (modéré) of "Fêtes" with their reorchestration later in the piece. What effect is achieved by the change in dynamics, instrumentation, and register?

ANALYSIS 7-1

Examine Examples 7-3 and 7-4. Play each example slowly, and then calculate the rise and fall of dissonance in it. Determine the relationship of consonance/dissonance between cadence points (resting points) at the end of a phrase and areas of activity within the phrase. In Example 7-4, examine the intervals formed by the two accompanying voices (bottom line), and then the intervals formed as these two voices combine with the melody.

Example 7-3.   **Stravinsky:** *The Five Fingers,* No. 6

Example 7-4.   **Stravinsky:** *The Five Fingers*, No. 4

etc.

E. Combination Tones

As we continue to study the nature of tones and their interaction, both harmonically (through intervals and chords) and melodically (through scales and melodies), we will become more aware that what we write is not all that we hear. There is a surface reality and a hidden reality in music. As composers, we write *one* tone—we *play/sing* it—and from the one tone there is suddenly a family of overtones. We then *write* an *interval*—we *play/sing* it—and the two tones generate *two* *families* of *overtones*, some related, others not. This phenomenon occurs in music as a result of *combination tones*. These are additional tones that result when an interval is played or sung. Some of these "extra" tones coincide with overtones and reinforce them. Others, however, sound below the actual interval; they either double one of its tones or sound as an entirely new tone.

Combination tones will be explored in Exercises 7-9 and 7-10. Listen to each interval to determine what "extra" tones you can *actually* hear.

EXERCISE 7-9

A   Play or sing with one or more of your classmates c and c′:

B Play or sing g and c':

C Play or sing c' and e':

D Play or sing c': half the class sings c' while the other half sings c'
sliding slowly to e':

E Play or sing c' and a':

F Repeat A–E, using a microphone to amplify the sound.

QUESTIONS AND
OBSERVATIONS

1 Were there differences between what you heard with amplification
and what you heard without it? Describe the differences.

2 Describe what happens when a rock group amplifies its music.
Would it sound the same without amplification? In addition to
altering the intensity of the sound (its loudness or softness), what
else does amplification do to the sound?

Some theorists consider combination tones unimportant since they
can rarely be heard. However, combination tones, whether heard faintly,
clearly, or not at all, do exist with the tones of the interval.

Combination tones can be produced on an electronic synthesizer,
as well as by the amplification of an interval.

EXERCISE
7-9D
(VARIATION)

If an electronic synthesizer is available, set up two unison tones
with the help of your teacher. Raise one tone gradually, using the ring
modulator. Compare the results with those of Exercise 7-9D.

There are two types of combination tones—*summation tones* and
difference tones. These are calculated as follows:

1   Summation tones: add the frequencies or frequency ratio of the two
    tones. For example, the summation tone of the perfect octave (whose
    frequency ratio is 2 to 1) is calculated as follows:

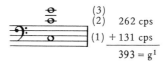

$$
\begin{array}{rl}
(3) & \\
(2) & 262 \text{ cps} \\
(1) & + 131 \text{ cps} \\
\hline
& 393 = g^1
\end{array}
$$

2   Difference tones: subtract the frequencies or frequency ratio of the
    bass tone from the soprano tone. For example, the difference tone of
    the perfect octave (2:1) is calculated as follows:

$$
\begin{array}{r}
262 \text{ cps} \\
- 131 \text{ cps} \\
\hline
131 = c
\end{array}
$$

EXERCISE 7-10

A. Using the C overtone series, calculate the combination tones (the
   summation tone and the difference tone) of:

   1. the perfect fifth (3:2):

   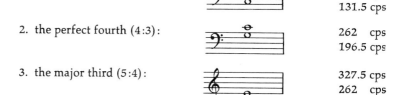

   196.5 cps
   131.5 cps

   2. the perfect fourth (4:3):

   262   cps
   196.5 cps

   3. the major third (5:4):

   327.5 cps
   262   cps

B. Play or sing examples 1–3.

ADDITIONAL
EXERCISES

1. Calculate the combination tones of:

   a minor third (6:5):

   a minor sixth (8:5):

a major six (10:6 = 5:3):

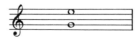

a major second (8:7 or 9:8):

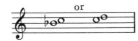

a minor second (16:15):

a minor seventh (7:4 or 16:9):

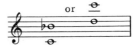

a major seventh (15:8):

2. Play a unison tone on your instrument joined by one of your class-mates; one holds the tone without vibrato while the other vibrates, increasing the amplitude of the vibrato. (Vary and/or amplify the dynamics.)
3. Play two high tones (M or m 2nd) forte, on a xylophone or other mallet instrument.

QUESTIONS AND OBSERVATIONS

1   Describe what you hear.
2   Do combination tones affect the consonant/dissonant character of an interval?
3   Which intervals contain difference tones that coincide with the fundamental tone C?
4   Describe the relationship of the combination tones of an interval to overtones of an interval. Where do they coincide? Where do they differ?
5   In some intervals, does one tone stand out, dominating the interval? If so which intervals?

F. Roots

Every interval can be considered as having one tone that dominates the interval and acts as its fundamental. This tone is the closest in relationship to the fundamental of the overtone series. In music, it can be in either the bass or soprano voice and is called the *root*. If we use intervals related to the C fundamental, the difference tone of the perfect fifth (♪) and major third (♪) reinforces the bass, which is the root. These consonant intervals are the most harmonically stable. The difference tone of the major second (♪) and minor seventh (♪) reinforces the bass, which is the root. But because of the harmonic ambivalence of the major second, which can relate to more than one fundamental (see below) and the minor seventh, whose root is weakened because of its distance from the fundamental of its overtone series, these more dissonant intervals are harmonically less stable.

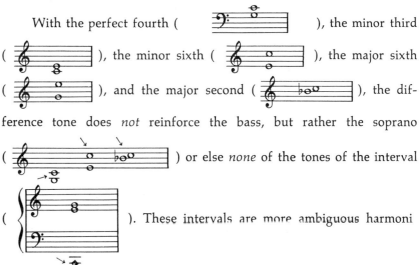

With the perfect fourth (♪), the minor third (♪), the minor sixth (♪), the major sixth (♪), and the major second (♪), the difference tone does *not* reinforce the bass, but rather the soprano (♪) or else *none* of the tones of the interval (♪). These intervals are more ambiguous harmoni

cally, and therefore less stable. With their root in the soprano, the perfect fourth, minor sixth, and major second (which can relate to various fundamentals) act like inversions. The minor third and the major sixth with its difference tone form a contradictory C major chord. In this case, we accept the bass of the minor third and the soprano of the major sixth as the root—a weaker, less dominant root, however, since it is not supported by its difference tone.

EXERCISE 7-11

A. Play or sing the intervals with one or· more of your classmates in Additional Exercise 1, pp. 75–76. (Transpose those that are too high.)

B. Transpose these intervals one or two octaves up or down.

C. Based on the sound of each interval and on your calculations, what would the root be of a:

   minor second?
   major seventh?
   minor seventh?

D. Would this *always* be the case?

E. Does register affect the degree of dominance of the root? The relative stability of the interval?

F. How could you use harmonically stable and unstable intervals in a piece?

ADDITIONAL
EXERCISES

A   Examine Exercises 6-7 and 6-8.

B   Is there a dominant tone in each interval? Which tone?

C   Are these dominant tones reinforced by combination tones? Which ones?

RESULTS

Compound intervals tend to act as simple intervals with regard to roots. However, the actual root can be weakened by the greater separation between the two tones of the interval. The bass, then, would tend to dominate and act as a root.

To Sum Up

Sounds other than the interval's two tones exist in the form of *overtones* and *combination tones*. These extra tones extend out—"up" and "down" in musical space—giving the interval a greater spatial presence and contributing to the quality of the interval and its consonant/dissonant character.

Combination tones can contribute to the stability of the interval by reinforcing one of its tones. Those intervals that are most stable harmonically are those whose root (doubled by a combination tone) is in the bass and close to the fundamental of the overtone series. Those intervals in which there is a remote relationship of the root to the fundamental, in which the root is in the soprano, or in which a root is not doubled by a combination tone tend to be harmonically less stable.

However, *musical context* (the manner in which intervals are related) will also influence the harmonic stability of the interval.

One tone played by a particular instrument has a particular quality. This tone quality, or timbre, is defined by the partials included in that tone. Two tones played by two instruments each have their own quality, but they also have a *combined* quality in which certain tones reinforce each other while others conflict. Two tones combined also contain *summation* and *difference tones*, extra tones that either reinforce the overtones present in the instrumental sound or add additional sounds. Dynamics, range, tempo, and duration (with its factors of attack and decay), in addition to the size and instrumentation of the interval, determine the interval's quality and affect its consonant/dissonant character.

Space must also be considered in determining the character of tones and intervals. Extending from the sound source, sound waves move equally throughout the enclosed space. Walls, chairs, people, and other impediments all absorb and reflect the sound, diminishing its energy.

The sound is prolonged while it decays, slowly or quickly, depending on its absorption or reverberation in the room. In the process, the quality of the sound and its consonant/dissonant character change.

Learning to measure these phenomena accurately would require a course in acoustics. But a general awareness of how tones interact in space is important in considering their effect as sound and their movement as music.

PROJECT 7-1

A. Write a short composition based on any interval (or group of intervals) and their spatial extensions (including transpositions and inversions) for a set or family of instruments (two violins; one viola and one cello; two recorders; etc.). Give special attention to the root movement of intervals in the way they relate and connect.

B. Have the piece played by two different instruments of the same family or by different families. Compare the sound and effect of the two performances. (Review the various families of instruments. Do you know their approximate range?)

PROJECT 7-2

A   Add a second vocal line above or below Example 7-5, using simple and compound, stable and unstable intervals. Keep in mind their consonant/dissonant character and the root movement of the intervals you select. Use dynamics and duration to contribute to the development and tension of the piece. Extend the piece to include one or more additional phrases so that the result is a short but balanced composition.

B   Transpose your piece up, starting on F♯.

C   Transpose (invert) the top line down an octave. Is the piece rec-
    ognizable? Why? Why not?

Example 7-5.   Vocal line

PROJECT 7-3

Using Example 6-5 as the bass, write a soprano with simple and
compound intervals. You can derive the soprano from any form of the
row (O, I, R, RI), skipping tones in various ways ($\frac{1}{1}\ \frac{3}{4}\ \frac{5}{7}$ etc.) and combining them. Root movement should be considered in regard to both
simple and compound intervals.

ANALYSIS 7-2

Find the root movement in Example 7-3 and the two lower parts of
Example 7-4. Do the roots move in a particular direction or to particular
tones in the piece? Describe the movement. Observe areas of relative
activity and inactivity. Where do these occur in the phrase?

LISTENING
SUGGESTIONS

J. S. Bach: Invention No. 1
Leonin: *Judaea and Jerusalem*

Observe the movement of intervals and their roots.

Dallapiccola: *Quaderno Musicale di Annalibera, 7*

Observe the movement of intervals and chords in various registers
and the changing texture created by combinations of two, three, and
more tones.

8 THE CHORD: The Triad

OBJECTIVES

1. To *construct* simple triads in root position and first and second inversions.

2. To *recognize* the tonal tendencies of chords in order to resolve and connect chords in simple three-voice pieces.

CAPSULE DEFINITIONS

Triad	A three-tone chord built on thirds.
Types of triads	Major, minor, diminished, augmented.
Chord positions	Root position, first inversion, second inversion.

 a symbol of a triad in root position.

 a symbol of a triad in its first inversion.

 a symbol of a triad in its second inversion.

Closed position	A triad whose tones fall within the octave.
Open position	A triad whose tones extend beyond the octave.
Chord function	The relationship of one chord to another.
Chord progression	The movement of chords in time.
Common tones	Tones common to more than one chord.
Broken chords	Chords whose tones are played in succession rather than together.
Block chords	Chords whose tones are played together.

A. Preliminary Explorations

The next vertical extension into musical space beyond the interval is the *chord.* A chord has at least three tones. Any three (or more) tones sounded together ( ) as one sound event, or consecutively ( ) as two or more sound events (with one or more notes held over), form a chord.

The chord is the basic harmonic unit that results when:

1   three or more melodic parts sound simultaneously (Example 8-1).
2   a combination of one or two melodic parts and their accompanying intervals or chords sounds simultaneously (Examples 8-2–8-4).
3   a combination of three or more tones (two or more intervals) sound together (Examples 8-5 and 8-6).

Example 8-1.   **Wagner:** *Tristan and Isolde*, prelude, mm. 32–33

Example 8-2.   **Stravinsky:** *The Five Fingers*, No. 4, larghetto

Example 8-3.   **Dallapiccola:** *Quaderno Musicale Di Annalibera*, No. 1

82

Example 8-4.   **Bartók:** *Mikrokosmos*, Vol. 3, No. 69

Example 8-5.   **Brahms:** Symphony No. 3, first movement

Example 8-6.   **Belknap:** *Summer*

We can construct chords by combining various tones, or by combining various intervals. Chord texture is denser than interval texture and gives a greater sense of musical space.

EXERCISE 8-1

    A Examine Examples 8-1–8-6.

    B List the intervals contained in each chord.

    C Compare the various chords. Which chords contain the more dissonant intervals? Play them. Do they *sound* the most dissonant?

    D In which example is the chord texture the most dense? Does the density of texture contribute to the general consonant/dissonant effect and/or to the sense of musical space?

EXERCISE 8-2

    A Use any overtone series you have already written to construct five three-tone chords:

(1) use two intervals of superimposed thirds.

(2) use any three tones. (If necessary, transpose tones to place them within the same octave.)

B Play or sing each chord with your classmates.

C Note the specific intervallic makeup of each chord—for example,

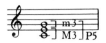

1 Describe the sound of the chords in Exercise 8-2A(1) in regard to their general quality (major, minor, etc.) and their consonant/dissonant character.

2 Describe the sound of the chords in Exercise 8-2A(2) in regard to their general quality and their consonant/dissonant character.

3 What is the essential difference between these two groups of chords?

4 Does one group sound more dissonant than the other?

Our ears and our knowledge of intervals should make us aware of three things:

1 There is a basic difference between the quality and consonant/dissonant character of chords built with thirds (including their inversions) and chords built with other tones or intervals.

2 Within each grouping of chords, there is a difference in the quality and the consonant/dissonant character of each chord. This difference depends on the specific intervallic makeup of each chord.

3 All chords contain a greater potential for dissonance than intervals because of the greater number and conflict of overtones and combination tones resulting from the several intervals in a chord.

On the basis of these observations we will designate three tone chords built on thirds as *simple chords* or *triads;* we will call other chords *complex chords.*

B. Simple Chords: The Triad

There are four kinds of triads that can be constructed:

Example 8-7.

EXERCISE 8-3

    A Number the internal structure of each interval within each triad in Example 8-7, each bass serving as tone *1*.

    B What are the differences in structure between:

        the major and minor triads?

        the major and augmented triads?

        the minor and diminished triads?

    C What gives each triad its identity?

    D Based on your knowledge of overtones and combination tones, grade each triad from the most consonant to the most dissonant.

    E Which triad is the most stable? The least stable? Why?

    F Transpose each chord in Example 8-7, using c′ as the bass to compare the interval structure of the four chords.

The structure and relationship of chords will be explored in Exercise 8-4. Each tone of the C major scale will be used as the bottom tone *1*, upon which chords will be constructed.

EXERCISE 8-4

    A Construct triads on each tone of the C major scale, using *only* those tones found in this scale.

    B Construct major triads on each tone of the C major scale, adding appropriate accidentals.

    C Repeat B, but construct minor triads.

    D Repeat B, but construct augmented triads.

    E Repeat B, but construct diminished triads.

F Play or sing each triad in A–E.

G Name and number each triad in A–E below the staff; use large Roman numerals (I) for major and augmented triads and small Roman numerals (i) for minor and diminished triads. In C major, for example, a C major chord would be I and a d minor chord would be ii.

H Using Arabic numerals (1), number each interval in A–E above the staff, starting with the bass in each triad.

I Mark all alterations (♯ or ♭) next to the tone numeral that has been changed—for example, $\frac{5♯}{3}$ or $\frac{5}{3♭}$.
$\qquad\qquad\qquad\qquad\qquad\quad\; \frac{}{1}\quad\;\; \frac{}{1}$

J Mark all alterations next to the chord numeral of augmented and diminished triads in D and E—for example I♯ or VII♭.

RESULTS   The chordal vocabulary of the seventeenth through the nineteenth centuries consists basically of the four simple chords in Example 8-7. The chord numerals in Exercise 8-4G represent the chord *relationships* in C major. The relationship of each chord in any key is determined by the tones 1–7 of that key.

Each of these triads in Example 8-7 has its own identity, which is based on the arrangement of its intervals or interval structure. Augmented and diminished triads are less stable harmonically than major or minor triads and are more dissonant, the fifth being augmented or diminished. The minor triad, which contains a perfect fifth, is more stable. However, its bottom interval of a minor third is less stable than a major third because the difference tones of the minor third conflict.

Perhaps in recognition of the conflict inherent in minor triads, Baroque composers often resolved a piece in a minor key by cadencing in the parallel major by raising the third (see Example 8-8).

Example 8-8.   **J. S. Bach:** Sinfonia VII

PROJECT 8-1

Use any of the triads you constructed in Exercise 8-4 in *any* order to write an interesting harmonic progression. Experiment by connecting one chord with various chords. Listen to the sound of the chords and the movement they create before deciding on the harmonies for your progression.

PROJECT 8-2

A   Take a folk song in C major. Compose a setting for piano in which the melody is the bass (♯or♭) upon which triads are constructed. Use any of the triads you constructed in Exercise 8-4 that would be appropriate to accompany the bass melody in the upper parts (⁵♯₃₁ ♪). Use these triads to create movement—tension and resolution.

B   Take the same folk song. Compose a piece in which the melody is the soprano (⁵₃♭¹₁ ♪). Harmonize, using *block* or *broken* triads in the lower parts (𝄢). Derive these triads from Exercise 8-4. Both melody and harmony tones should be 1, 3, or 5 of the chord. To create smoother chord connections, you can double the tones of the triad when necessary and use the various types of motion—contrary, oblique, similar, and parallel—in moving from voice to voice and chord to chord.

ANALYSIS 8-1

A. Bartók: *Mikrokosmos*, Vol. 3, No. 69
   1. Play each part separately, then together, slowly.
   2. List the major, minor, diminished, and augmented triads in the piece.
   3. Which melody tones do *not* belong in the triad?
B. Legrant: Credo, No. 56 (*Historical Anthology of Music*, Vol. I, Fifteenth Century)

   1. Play the piece slowly.
   2. List the various triads in the piece.
   3. Where there is not a complete triad, list the interval.

LISTENING
SUGGESTIONS

Beethoven: Symphony No. 3, I
Mozart: Symphony No. 40, I

Observe the use of block chords and broken chords. Which chords act as "foreground"? Which act as "background"?

C. Chord Spacing: Chords in *Root* Position

(in *closed* and *open* position)

Each of the chords considered thus far has been in *root* position. Diminished and augmented triads, which are less stable and more ambiguous harmonically, depend on musical context to strengthen their weak roots (such as an unstable interval moving to a stable interval).

EXERCISE 8-5

A   List the various forms of the C major triad contained in the overtone series. (refer to example 3-2, pg. 25).
B   Which triads fall within the octave?
C   Which extend beyond the octave?

RESULTS

When all three tones of a chord fall *within* the octave, the chord is in *closed* position; in this case, the chord is comparable to simple intervals. When one or two tones of a chord extend *beyond* the octave, the chord is in *open* position; in this case, the chord is a combination of compound and simple intervals.

D. Changing From Closed To Open Position

EXERCISE 8-6

A   Take the C major triad in closed position. Keep the root but spread the upper voices to open position.

B   Play or sing the various forms of the triad with your classmates noting the differences in their sounds.

C   Mark the intervals included in each triad.

EXERCISE 8-7

A   Take the C major triad in closed position. Keep the root as the bass, but transpose any voice up or down to open position.

B   Play or sing the example, noting the differences in its sounds.

C   Mark the intervals of each triad.

D   Describe the motion (parallel, similar, oblique, or contrary) of each voice from one position to another position of the triad.

E   Transpose A so that the F♯ is the root tone.

QUESTIONS AND
OBSERVATIONS

1   Do the C major triads in Exercises 8-6 and 8-7 sound the same?

2   Describe the similarities and the differences among these triads.

3   In which positions does each triad sound most stable? Why?

4   Where is the root in relation to the other tones of the triad in each position?

Changes of *interval structure* within each chord resulting from a change in position will somewhat alter the overtone and combination-tone structure and therefore the character of the chord.

E. Chord Spacing: Inversions of Chords

All triads that are *not* in root position are called *inversions*, or *inverted chords*. All chords (and intervals) can be inverted. But each inversion alters the character of the chord, for it changes the interval structure within the chord. The change is greater with inverted chords, in which the root is not in the bass, than with root-position chords that move from closed to open position.

EXERCISE 8-8

A   Take the C major triad in closed position (chord 1 in the example), and transpose the root up one octave, holding the third and fifth.

B   Take the resulting chord (2) and transpose the third (e′) up one octave.

C   Once again, take the C major triad; this time, transpose the fifth (g¹) down one octave, holding the root and third.

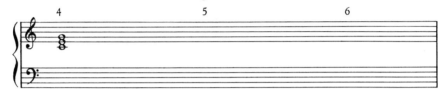

D   Take the resulting chord (5) and transpose the third (e¹) down one octave.

E   Write other versions of each inverted chord in open position.

F   Play or sing chords 1–6, and describe the character of each. Do some of the chords sound more stable than the others?

G   Mark the intervals of each triad. Are some inversions more stable than others? Which ones? Why?

H   Compare the sound of the triads in root position (closed or open) with the sound of their inversions (closed or open). Is there a basic difference?

I   Which group tends to be more stable, the root-position chords or the inverted chords? Why?

 In Exercise 8-8, A and D, the third (e) is in the bass:

A. Closed

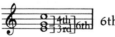

D. Open

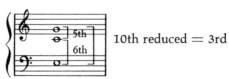

Any triad with the third in the bass is called a *first-inversion chord* or simply a *sixth* chord. The important interval that gives this inverted chord its identity is the interval from the bass to the root, which is always a sixth (or its compound form, a thirteenth) in open or closed position.

Second Inversion In Exercise 8-8, B and C, the fifth (g) is in the bass:

B. Closed

C. Closed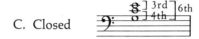

Any triad with the fifth in the bass is called a *second-inversion chord* or simply a *six-four chord*. The important interval that gives this inverted chord its identity is the interval from the bass to the root, which is always a fourth (or its compound form, an eleventh) in open or closed position.

Although each inversion, with its particular bass, alters the character of a chord, the root of a chord remains the same no matter where it is positioned in the chord. A C major triad, whether it be in root position ⑤③① or in first ⑥ or second ⑥④ inversion, is *always* a C major triad.

EXERCISE 8-9

A Write a version of Exercise 8-4A in
   1. first inversion in closed position.
   2. first in open position.
   3. second inversion in closed position.
   4. second in open position.
   5. a combination of inversions and root-position chords in open and closed position, using contrary, oblique, similar, and parallel motion. Add a fourth voice, doubling a tone of the triad when it can help to make smoother chord connections—for example,

B Circle the roots of each chord in A5.
C Play or sing A5.
D Revise A5, altering triads and changing voice leading if this makes A5 more effective harmonically as it progresses from chord to chord.

E   Play or sing D backwards (retrograde) with your classmates.

F   Write another version of Exercise 8-4, using the descending C major scale as the soprano.

G   Transpose A5 or F up one octave; down one octave.

H   Describe the chords in the different registers.

I   Mark each chord in A5 and F as follows:  for root position, for first inversion, and for second inversion.

To Sum Up   All triads change their character to some degree if tones within the chord are transposed up or down from one position to another (open to closed, or vice versa). If the change is from root position to its inversion, the degree of character change is more pronounced, but a C major chord, in whatever position, is always a C major chord. A change from a C major chord to a C minor chord is still a greater alteration of character than any change within a C major chord. The greatest change, of course, is the movement of one chord to an entirely different chord.

Inversions tend to be less stable harmonically than chords in root position. In the first and second inversion of chords, less stable intervals tend to move or resolve to more stable intervals in the chord (see Example 8-9).

Example 8-9.   First and second inversion chords

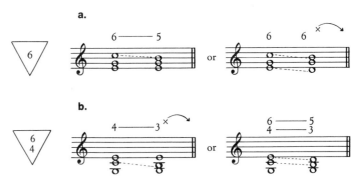

Observe, however, that while the less stable interval moves or resolves to its neighbor in the next chord, the other tone either remains stationary or moves to its neighbors in the next chord. In doing so, it can create other unstable intervals within the chord that will also suggest resolution.

EXERCISE 8-10

Resolve those chords in Examples 8-9 and 8-10 that contain relatively unstable (X) intervals to chords that contain more stable intervals.

Example 8-10.   First and second inversion chords

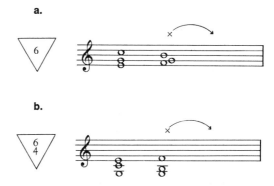

F. Chord Progressions: Common Tones

A diatonic scale has seven different tones. Triads built on the diatonic scale have seven different roots. Each of the seven triads shares the available seven tones. Each triad can be altered by the substitution of new tones. The number of tones used however cannot exceed the twelve tones of the chromatic scale.

Those tones shared by different triads are called *common tones.* These tones will occur in different positions in different triads. For

example  e′ and g′ are common

to the c major and e minor triad but they appear in different positions. *Common tones* can remain stationary as one chord moves to another chord.

EXERCISE 8-11

A Which of the seven chords in Exercise 8-4A have:
1. two tones in common?
2. one tone in common?
3. no tones in common?
B Do adjacent chords (such as I and ii) have common tones?
C What is the relationship between chords with one tone in common? Two tones in common?

The movement of one chord to other chords is called a *harmonic progression.* A harmonic progression creates a sense of musical motion.

EXERCISE 8-12

Write two versions of the following progressions in three parts in C major. Write version I in root position and version II in root and first inversion. (Keep common tones in the same part for smooth voice leading.)

A   Two tones in common: I(C), VI(a), IV(F), and II(d) chords.
B   One tone in common: I(C), V(G), II(d), and VI(a) chords.
C   Combine A and B, making an interesting harmonic progression.

RESULTS   Chord progressions with one or two common tones flow more smoothly, creating less tension than chords with no common tones. Greater tension is created when all the voices within a chord move to another chord than when one or two voices remain stationary.

G. Chord Progressions: Voice Leading

Each tone of an interval moves or resolves to a tone of the next interval. *Intervallic tension* is harmonic and melodic. The three or more tones of a chord move or resolve to the tones of the next chord. *Chordal tension* is harmonic (within the chord) and melodic (between the chords). More dissonant chords tend to move or resolve to less dissonant chords. The more dissonant intervals within the chord tend to move or resolve to less dissonant intervals (see Examples 8-9 and 8-10).

We observed that chords with tones in common create less tension in their melodic flow. Chords with no tones in common can also be treated as smooth-flowing melodic progressions with little tension if all the voices move in a parallel direction. But if the various voices in a chord move in different directions, the melodic progressions create a greater sense of musical motion, tension, and variety of texture because of the changing relationships of intervals *within* the chord.

H. Chord Progressions: Harmonization

Chords consist of tones and intervals arranged *vertically* (spatially) that move or resolve *horizontally* (temporally) as harmony in the form of soprano, bass, and other parts. A harmonic progression is the composite texture of these various parts. The following general guidelines should help you extend a harmonic progression beyond a few chords and harmonize a melody or bass part in a tonal style.

1. If a soprano or bass part is given, you must first determine the scale upon which it is based and the number of sharps (♯) or flats (♭) in that scale. (The interval structure of the C major scale, with its related chords, is your model.)

2. A given soprano or bass part should complement the added bass or soprano part. Skips could be balanced in the added part by stepwise motion in contrary, similar, oblique, or, on rare occasions, parallel motion.

3. The added bass part should use consonant intervals that could serve as the root, third, and, on rare occasions, the fifth of the chord. The added soprano should use predominantly consonant intervals (1, 3, 5, 6) with occasional dissonant intervals (2, 7) that move or resolve to more consonant intervals. (Keep the basic chords in mind.)

4. See what tones are then missing from the chord, and write your inner part(s) with these tones. Double one tone of the chord in four-part harmonization, but in three-part harmonization do this only when necessary for smooth voice leading. Tones common to successive chords could be kept in the same voice. (In major and minor triads, the root is doubled most often. The third or fifth can occasionally be doubled for smooth voice leading.)

5. The range of each voice should not exceed an interval of a twelfth:

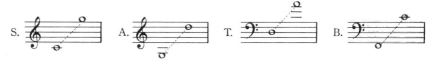

In simple pieces, even this range would be extreme. The distance between soprano and alto, or alto and tenor, should normally be no larger than one octave.

EXERCISE 8-13

A Play Examples 8-11–8-14.

B Describe or mark the various types of motion between the various parts.

C Describe the effect of the various types of motion—for example, the parallel motion in Example 8-12 and the skip and stepwise motion in Examples 8-11, 8-12, and 8-14.

D What tones are common to successive chords? How are these tones treated?

Example 8-11.   Harmonization

Example 8-12.   Harmonization

Example 8-13.   Harmonization

Example 8-14.   Harmonization

E Take the soprano of Example 8-11 and write your own three-part harmonization. Take the bass of Example 14 and write your own four-part harmonization.

PROJECT 8-3

A Take the melody of a folk or popular song. Use major and minor chords (augmented and diminished chords rarely) and block or broken chords in various positions as an accompaniment for piano or guitar and voice, or another accompanying instrument and voice.

Interpret the *meaning* of the words with your setting of the song.

B   Repeat A, but write for two or three voices (instrumental accompaniment optional), stressing the connection from chord to chord and from tone to tone within each chord.

C   Write a short piece for piano, voices, varied instruments, or a combination of these. Use major and minor triads (augmented and diminished triads rarely, if at all) in open and/or closed position, in root position first inversion (second inversion rarely, if at all) and in the same register, expanding the range occasionally—and with care. Each chord should relate to the next chord. You can vary dynamics and duration in order to help create an interesting chord "texture." Also, you can double tones of a triad in order to give it extra weight, or to aid in voice leading.

ANALYSIS 8-2   **Beethoven:** *Piano Sonata*, Op. 2, No. 1, second movement, m. 1–8

Observe the use of chords in root, first, and second position.

A   Name each chord and/or mark chord numerals under it.
B   Put interval numbers above each chord.
C   Circle common tones.
D   Which chords are used most frequently?
E   Where are chords in first position used?
F   Where are chords in second position used?
G   Which chords are in open position? Which are in closed position?
H   In four-voice chords, which tone of the triad is doubled?
I   What types of motion are used in the movement from chord to chord?

Mozart: Symphony No. 40, I
Beethoven: Symphony No. 3, I
J. S. Bach: *Musical Offering,* trio sonata

Observe the types and positions of triads used, their spacing, and their movement. Observe the relationship between melody and harmony, foreground and background.

I. Broken Chords

As a vertical sound event, a chord can be extended in time by being "broken" up into smaller horizontal groupings. A triad with three tones can be broken into two () or three () sound events, each interval or tone having a life of its own.

Melodies can be made from broken chords (Examples 8-15 and 8-16).

Example 8-15.   **Beethoven:** *Violin Concerto*, third movement

Example 8-16.   **Brahms:** *Violin Concerto*, first movement

In addition, accompaniment motives can be made from broken chords (Examples 8-17–8-20).

Example 8-17.   **Mozart:** *Piano Sonata*, K. 545, first movement

Example 8-18.   **Stravinsky:** *The Five Fingers*, No. 5, moderato

Example 8-19.   **Stravinsky:** *The Five Fingers*, No. 6, Lento

Example 8-20.   "Amazing Grace," from *The Southern Harmony*

etc.

Each accompanying motive is short, lasting only a few beats. But each is extended by repetition—exact or sequential—as the chords change.

Each is limited in range, falling within the compass of the hand or voice, because each is written for the piano, violin, or voice.

But one is not limited to the compass of the hand. Consider Examples 8-21 and 8-22.

Example 8-21.   **Beethoven:** *Piano Sonata*, Op. 106, first movement

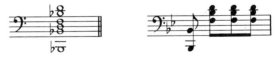

Example 8-22.   **Brahms:** *Symphony No. 4*, first movement

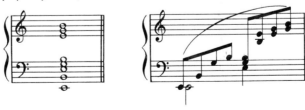

Voice leading of chords is somewhat more flexible in piano style than in vocal music. Tones within the chord can move to their neighbor in the next chord but are not *obliged* to.

PROJECT 8-4

Using broken chords, write or rewrite an accompaniment to any project in Chapter 8.

ANALYSIS 8-3

A. Examine each of the accompaniment motives in Examples 8-17–8-22. Diagram the voice leading (from tone to tone) in the accompaniment.
B. Look for other examples of accompanying motives based on the broken chord in:
1. Beethoven: Piano sonatas, Vol. I
2. Folk or popular music (with piano, guitar, etc.)

LISTENING
SUGGESTIONS

Schubert: "Das Wandern," from *Die schöne Müllerin*
Queen: "Love of My Life," from *A Night at the Opera*
Mozart: Piano Sonata, K. 545, first movement
Beethoven: Piano Sonata, Op. 2, No. 1, second movement

Observe the types and elaboration (extension through repetition or variation) of the accompaniment motives.

9 COMPLEX CHORDS: Nontriadic

OBJECTIVES

1. To *construct* three-tone chords with their inversions, based on various intervals.

2. To *recognize* the relationship between triadic and nontriadic chords built on various intervals—their root relationship and their tonal tendencies—in order to resolve and connect various chords in simple pieces.

CAPSULE DEFINITIONS

Complex chord	Any chord of three or more tones that is *not* built on thirds.
Types of complex chords	Chords built on fifths and fourths, sevenths and seconds, and combinations of various mixed intervals.

A. Preliminary Explorations

Composers in the seventeenth through the nineteenth centuries wrote music based on a tonal system of key and chord relationships. Twentieth-century composers have either extended, transformed, or abandoned this system. Whereas triads are the essential chordal vocabulary of tonal music, extended triads and nontriads (chords built on other intervals—seconds, fourths, fifths, and so on) constitute a part of the twentieth-century chordal vocabulary.

Chords built with intervals other than thirds generally have a more complex overtone and combination-tone structure and therefore tend to be more dissonant than triads. But we know that dynamics, instrumentation, duration, register, and musical context—in *addition* to the chord's structure—can affect the consonant/dissonant character of any chord.

B. Complex Chords: Three-Tone Chords Based on The Perfect Fifth and Perfect Fourth

The chord most related to the triad is the chord based on the perfect fifth (partials 4/6/9:). The related chord based on the perfect fourth (partials 9/12/16, reduced one octave:) is the less stable second inversion of the chord of fifths.

In the following exercises in Chapter 9, various complex chords with different interval structures will be explored.

Exercise 9-1

    A Sing or play Exercise 5-9C.

    B Add a perfect fifth above the top part of Exercise 5-9C in order to form a chord of perfect fifths; play or sing the result.

    C Repeat B, but add a fifth below the bottom part of Exercise 5-9C.

    D Add a fourth above the top part of Exercise 5-9D in order to form a chord of perfect fourths; play or sing the result.

    E Repeat D, but add a fourth below the bottom part of Exercise 5-9D.

    F Comment on the character of the chords in B–E, and compare them.

Three-tone chords built on perfect fifths form two incomplete triads.

EXERCISE 9-2

A   Construct *two* triads using the chord of the fifth by filling in the missing tones:

B   Play or sing with your classmates A as open fifths—then filled in as two triads.
C   Comment on the character of each chord in B, and compare them.
D   What is the most likely root of each?
E   What would the difference tone of the major ninth be?
F   Would the difference-tone strengthen c′ as the most likely root?

RESULTS

Chords built with perfect fifths sound mild in comparison with the filled-in two-triad version. The compound interval of a major ninth is spaced widely enough to be only mildly dissonant.

C′ would be the most likely root, even though the perfect fifth would have g as its root. The bottom fifth is in a stronger harmonic position because its difference tone, c, strengthens c′:

More interesting, and somewhat more ambiguous, is the chord built with perfect fourths.

EXERCISE 9-3

A   Play or sing the following example:

B   Compare the consonant/dissonant character of the two chords.
C   What is the most likely root of chord 2? Is there another possible root?

D   Complete the resolutions of chord 2:

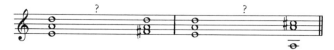

E   What are the most likely roots of each chord in D? (When there is more than one possible root, consider the musical context.)

EXERCISE 9-4

A   Mark the intervals above each chord in Example 9-1.
B   Mark the chord numerals below each triad.
C   Account for the tones that are *not* part of a triad.

Example 9-1.   A classical cadence in A major

RESULTS   As the chord vocabulary is increased, so too are the ambiguities and functions of chord roots. In Exercises 9-3D and 9-4, the chords built on fourths were not treated as independent chords. Instead, they were treated as an extension of the triad in a tonal context (D and A major). The interval of the fourth was treated melodically as a nonchord tone that resolved to a chord tone, the third. What other intervals required a resolution in Example 9-1?

Some twentieth-century music treats the chord of the fourth as an independent chord that requires no such resolution. Consider Examples 9-2 and 9-3.

Example 9-2.   **Bartók:** *Concerto for Orchestra*, second movement, mm. 200–202

Example 9-3.   **Bartók:** *Concerto for Orchestra,* introduction, mm. 22–27

EXERCISE 9-5

A   Using the C major scale as a bass, construct chords of fourths with the seven tones of that scale. Play or sing the chords.

B   Alter the soprano of A so that each chord consists only of *perfect fourths.* Play or sing the resulting chords.

C   Compare the chords in A and B. Which chords in A are more dissonant? Which in B? Why? What is the most likely root of these chords?

EXERCISE 9-6

A   Using the seven tones of the C major scale as a bass, construct chords of fifths moving to chords of fourths.

B   Resolve each chord of fourths | to a triad. Add a fourth tone (the root of the triad) when needed.

C   Delay each resolution with an intervening   (∧)   chord.

D   Use accidentals to alter the chords of A so that each chord consists only of perfect fifths and perfect fourths.

E   Would the resolutions in B and C "work" with these altered chords?

C. Chords Based on Perfect Fifths and Perfect Fourths: Inversions

All chords can be inverted. All inverted chords change their character to some degree. Complex chords increase the ambiguity of their identity and their root with inversion.

EXERCISE 9-7

A Invert the chord of perfect fifths to:
1. its first inversion, transposing the c′ up one octave.
2. its second inversion.
3. its third inversion.
B Play 1, 2, and 3.

EXERCISE 9-8

A Invert the chord of perfect fourths to:
1. its first inversion, transposing the d′ up one octave.
2. its second inversion.
B Play 1 and 2.

QUESTIONS AND
OBSERVATIONS

1 Do the inversions sound similar to the original?
2 Determine the most likely root of each of the chords. Are these roots the same?
3 Which inversions of the perfect fourth and perfect fifth are similar?
4 Which are the most stable forms of each chord? Why?

Each inversion creates a new chord of mixed intervals. The character of each new chord is therefore quite different. So is its root. Chords that contain more dissonant intervals (such as minor ninths and diminished fifths) will be more dissonant. Chords with ambiguous roots and harmonic instability suggest resolution to more stable chords. The composer, however, can delay or impede any resolution for the purpose of creating a musical effect.

D. Chords Based on the Second and the Seventh

When inverted, chords of the fifth and fourth contain ninths and sevenths as well as seconds.

Chords based on the major second (partials 8/9/10,

reduced one octave:), and its complete inversion, the chord based on the minor seventh (partials 5/9/16:), retain

their relationship to the triad since both contain the interval of a third (simple and compound form).

EXERCISE 9-9

A Invert the chord of major seconds to its other possible positions.

B Play or sing each version.
C Compare the sound of the various versions.
D Has the character of each chord changed as a result of inversion? Describe.
E What is the root of each of the chords? Why?
F Flat the e and play or sing the altered version.
G Has the character of the original version changed with the alteration? Describe.
H Which is the best interval "harmonically"? Which is most related to the triad?
I Transpose the upper tones of the chord in root position to form a chord of ninths. Play this and compare it with the original chord of seconds.

The chord built with minor sevenths (partials 5/9/16:)

is less dense than the chord of seconds. It has more than one possible root. Name them.

Like the chord of the fifth, this chord can be texturally enriched if other tones are added.

Exercise 9-10

A Write two versions of the chord of minor sevenths (refer to the chord of fourths and the chord of fifths), using a different interval in each to "fill in" and enrich the chord.

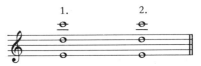

B Play both versions.
C Which sounds denser and more dissonant?

Exercise 9-11

A Complete this short three-part "chorale," using at least five chords in root position of the minor seventh, major second, perfect fifth, and perfect fourth spaced in open and closed position.

B Mark each chord (seventh, second, etc.).
C Use accidentals (♯, ♭) with care.
D Circle each root.
E Play or sing the piece with one or more of your classmates. Which point in the phrase is most consonant? Most dissonant? Why?
F Examine the chord progression for voice leading.
G Revise A, using inversions in open and closed position to create smoother progressions.

E. Spacing: Open and Closed Position

It is harder to talk of the open and closed position of three-tone complex chords, because some of these chords already extend beyond the octave: for example, ⎰ and ⎰ . But through transposition and inversion, *closed-position chords* can be opened up.

Exercise 9-12

Transpose any voice in Exercise 9-6B so as to form *open*-position chords.

QUESTIONS AND OBSERVATIONS

1 Does changing a complex chord's position (closed or open) change its character? Why?
2 Does changing its position change its root?
3 Does a change of position (closed or open) with the same bass alter the chord's character as much as its inversion with a changed bass? Why? (Would a triad be affected in the same way as a complex chord?)
4 What is the basic difference between simple and complex chords?
5 Do alterations, changes of position, and inversion affect the root of the triad to the same degree that they affect the root(s) of the complex chord? Explain.

Besides the essential differences, there are some similiarities between the structure of triads and the structure of the complex chords we examined.

Some complex chords occur as *incomplete* triads:

Their roots are fairly easy to define.

Both types of chords undergo *some* change of structure and character when inverted. The change is more marked in complex chords. Roots, which remain constant with inversions of triads, will more likely change with inversions of complex chords.

All chords based on a specific interval (thirds, fourths, fifths, and so on) change their interval structure with inversion.

Project 9-1

Transpose A or G in Exercise 9-11 to another pitch level, and develop it into a more extended piece. For variety of texture and elaboration of the shape-form use voices and/or instruments and/or piano in different registers, and with different dynamics. (Refer to Bach's *Organ Works*, Vol. VI: "*Allein Gott in der Höh' sei Ehr'*," Nos. 3 and 4, and "*Gottes Sohn ist Kommen*," No. 25.)

PROJECT 9-1
(VARIATION)

Compose a three-part choralelike piece, "resolving" complex chords to triads when appropriate. Use inversions and closed and open positions. For variety of texture and elaboration of the shape-form, follow the suggestions offered in Project 9-1.

PROJECT 9-2

Compose a dramatic piece with complex chords, adding more intervals to enrich the chord if you wish. Write the piece for piano and/or a family of instruments (strings, winds, or brasses). (Optional: use percussion instruments to accent your chords, or as a counterpoint to them.)

ANALYSIS 9-1

A. Play Schoenberg's *Six Little Piano Pieces,* Op. 19, No. 6.
 1. Mark the intervals of each chord.
 2. (a) Indicate the type of chord: triad or complex chord.
  (b) When possible, indicate the kind of chord—for example, perfect fourth.
 3. Circle the most likely root of each chord.
 4. Does there appear to be any *relationship* of roots? If so, what?
B. Play Stravinsky's *The Five Fingers,* No. 4. Refer to your analysis of this piece in Chapter 7.
 1. (a) Indicate the type of chord.
  (b) When possible, indicate the kind of chord: E minor sixth chord or chord of the fourth (perfect fourth or augmented fourth).
 2. Circle the most likely root of each chord.
 3. Describe the relationship of roots (step-skip to other roots).
 4. On what scale is this piece based?

LISTENING
SUGGESTIONS

Bartók: Concerto for Orchestra, introduction
Hindemith: Octet for Clarinet and String Quartet, first movement
Hindemith: *Mathis der Maler* (symphony), second movement

Fine: *Paeon*

Note the use of triads and perfect fourth chords. How does each composer use each type of chord?

10 CHORD EXTENSIONS: Chords of Four or More Tones

OBJECTIVES

1. To *construct* chords of four or more tones, with their inversions, based on intervals derived from scale forms and other sources, including the twelve-tone row.

2. To *recognize* the consonant/dissonant quality of these chords in relation to triads and other three-voice chords in order to resolve and connect various chords in different ways.

CAPSULE DEFINITIONS

Twelve-tone row	A melodic arrangement of the twelve tones of the chromatic scale.
Different forms of the twelve-tone row	*original (O):* as above.
	inversion (I): upside down.
	retrograde (R): backward
	retrograde inversion (RI): backward and upside down.
"Mirror" form	An inversion (upside-down version) of a melody or harmony.
Non-chord tones	Tones that embellish but do not belong to the chord.

A. Preliminary Explorations

Extended chords can be formed by combining four or more tones or by combining various intervals. An extended chord results when:

1 one or more tones are added to a triad (Examples 10-1–10-3).
2 one or more tones are added to a three-tone complex chord (Examples 10-4 and 10-5).

Example 10-1. **Debussy:** *Nocturnes,* I

Example 10-2. **Beethoven:** *Symphony No. 9,* fourth movement, beginning

Example 10-3. **Mahler:** *Symphony No. 10,* first movement, mm. 203–6

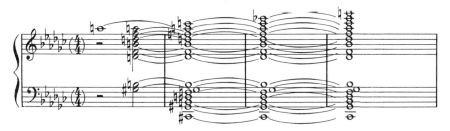

Example 10-4.   Yannatos: *Cycles*, third movement

Example 10-5.   Schoenberg: *Six Little Piano Pieces*, Op. 19, 3 (two excerpts)

EXERCISE 10-1

A   Examine Examples 10-1–10-5.
B   List the basic triads in Examples 10-1–10-3.
C   List the intervals and additional triads in these three examples.
D   List the intervals contained in the complex chords in Examples 10-4 and 10-5.
E   Compare each chord in regard to its interval structure. Which chords are more dissonant? Why?

B. Triadic Extensions

As one or more tones are added to a triad, its interval structure becomes more complex and its character and consonant/dissonant quality change.

In Exercises 10-2 and 10-3, and the "Additional Exercises" that

follow, triads will be extended with various intervals to create chords
of four or more tones. Observe the changes that occur in the sound of
each new chord.

EXERCISE 10-2

Take an exercise or project from Chapter 8.

A   Add one (or more) tone(s) (seconds, fourths, or sixths) to the various
    triads in root position.
B   Play or sing the new version.
C   Do the triads maintain their character when new tones are added?
D   Examine the new interval structure of the chords. Do they remain
    basically the same chord with the same root?
E   Rewrite A. Invert chords when necessary for smoother voice leading.

EXERCISE 10-3

Take the same exercise or project from Chapter 8 that you used
above.

A   Add sevenths (from the root).
B   Add ninths.
C   Add elevenths.
D   Add thirteenths.
E   Play each version.
F   What triads are now contained in each example?
G   What are the roots of these extended triads? Why?
H   Reduce D so as to make each tone fall within the octave.
 I   Write other versions of D (inversions and reductions) that are *not*
    confined to the octave.
 J   Play and compare the sound of the versions in H and I.
K   Do the roots remain the same with inversion and reduction? Is there
    a best root? (Compare with F.)
L   Explain the various versions of thirteenth chords. Are they simple or
    complex chords?

ADDITIONAL
EXERCISES

1. A. Construct a diminished triad on c', and add an additional minor
      third (a diminished seventh from the root).

B. Take 1A and add an additional minor third (diminished ninth from the root).

2.   Construct an augmented triad on c′, and add an additional major third (an augmented seventh from the root).

3. A. Construct a minor triad on c′, and add an additional minor third (a minor seventh from the root).

B. Add an additional minor third (minor ninth from the root) to 3A.

C. Add an additional major third (major ninth from the root) to 3A.

4. A. Construct a major triad on c′, and add an additional major third (a major seventh from the root).

B. Add a minor third (a major ninth from the root) to 4A.

C. Alter the ninth in 4B, making it a minor ninth.

D. Construct a major triad on c′, and add an additional minor third (a minor seventh from the root).

E. Add a major third (a major ninth from the root) to 4D.

5.   Make other alterations so as to create other seventh and ninth chords.

Play the various forms of these chords. Comment on the relationship of each chord to the *original* chord—in terms of character, roots, and stability.

RESULTS   When new tones are added to the triad, the distinction between simple and complex chords becomes blurred. Inversion and alteration change the interval structure of the extended triad. The more complex the extended triadic chord (see Exercise 10-3, G and H), the greater its dissonance, the less clear its interval structure, and the more ambiguous its root. The increased number of partials and combination tones resulting from other tones besides the root contributes to this root ambiguity in the extended triadic chord.

C. Complex Chord Extensions

*Chords of
the Fourth*

EXERCISE 10-4

A   Add a perfect fourth above (or below) the various chords of the fourth in Exercise 9-1, D or E.

B   Add another perfect fourth above (or below) these chords.

C   Add still another perfect fourth above (or below).

D   Play each of these versions.

E   Reduce C so as to make each tone fit within an octave.

F   Write other versions of E (inversions and reductions) that are *not* confined to the octave.

G   Play and compare the sound of the versions in E and F.

H   Is there a best root in each version?

*Chords of
the Fifth,
Second,
and Seventh*

EXERCISE 10-4
(VARIATIONS)

1   Add perfect fifths above (or below) the various chords of the fifth in Exercise 9-1, B or C. Then repeat steps B–H of Exercise 10-4.

2   Add major seconds above (or below) the various chords of the second in Exercise 5-9K. Then repeat steps B–H of Exercise 10-4.

3   Add minor sevenths above (or below) the various chords of the seventh in Exercise 5-9N. Then repeat steps B–H of Exercise 10-4.

4   Change the structure of the complex chords in 1–3 and/or in Exercise 10-4. Use accidentals to form chords of the minor second, major seventh, augmented fourth, diminished fifth, or combinations of these with the intervals of the chords already used (chords of the major or minor second, perfect or augmented fourth, and so on).

QUESTIONS AND
OBSERVATIONS

1   Is it difficult to spell and to hear altered chords? (Review those intervals that contain accidentals. Give particular attention to augmented and diminished intervals that present problems.)

2   How far can you extend a triad within C major—for example, starting on c′ and adding major and minor triads—before returning to the original tone transposed?

3   How far can you extend a diminished triad, starting on c′ and adding minor thirds, before returning to the original tone transposed?

4   How far can you extend an augmented triad, starting on c′ and adding major triads, before returning to the original tone transposed?

5   How far can you extend the following chords, starting on c′, before returning to the original tone transposed?

A. chord of perfect fourths

B. chord of perfect fifths

C. chord of augmented fourths

D. chord of diminished fifths

6   How far can you extend the following chords, starting on c', before returning to the original tone transposed?

A. chord of major seconds

B. chord of minor sevenths

C. chord of minor seconds

D. chord of major sevenths

Each chord with a fixed interval structure contains a finite number of tones. We can extend chords by altering tones and mixing intervals. For example, we can extend a diminished triad by adding another diminished triad, placing a major third between each triad (Example 10-6). We can extend an augmented triad by adding another augmented triad, placing a minor third between each triad (Example 10-7).

Example 10-6.   Diminished triad

Example 10-7.   Augmented triad

No chord can contain more than twelve tones of the chromatic scale.

When new tones are added to complex chords, and/or when such chords are inverted and altered, they tend to become more dissonant and unstable and their roots are more ambiguous. (Exception: adding a third to a chord of perfect fifths, will clarify its structure and improve its stability giving added weight to its root, c'.) Both simple and complex extended chords that are reduced to the span of an octave will change their character and tend to lose their intervallic identity. A chord with many tones that has been reduced will sound like a tone cluster.

D. Other Chord Formations

Tone Clusters   Highly concentrated chords of major and/or minor seconds that result from the reduction of extended chords, or that are constructed, are called tone clusters. These chord formations can be confined to a particular register, or they can extend throughout many registers (Example 10-8). We can enlarge tone clusters further by adding non-

Example 10-8.

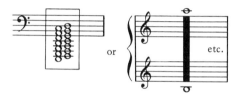

pitched sounds to the twelve tones of the chromatic scale. Any cluster of tones will be dissonant, and some will be more dissonant than others because they include more tones and/or are placed in the low register.

Derived   Simple and complex chords can be constructed from the tones of
Chords   any traditional or made-up scale.

EXERCISE 10-5

Using the *pentatonic* (five-tone) scale as a bass, construct:

A   triads.

B   various forms of complex chords.

C   chords that use *only* the five tones of the scale.

EXERCISE 10-6

Using any scale as a bass (see Chapter 17), construct triads that use only the tones of that scale.

The
Chromatic
Scale:
Twelve-Tone
Chord
"Formations"

The tones of the chromatic scale *not* included in the diatonic scale and its related harmonies in a particular key were used as *nonchord* tones in the tonal style of the seventeenth through nineteenth centuries. In the late nineteenth century, the chromatic scale was used melodically, harmonically, *and* tonally. Triads that had been extended to include *added* and *altered* tones could be built on *any* tone of the chromatic scale and could move more freely from key to key.

Twentieth-century composers have also used the flexible chromatic scale as a source of melodic and harmonic material because it offered them more tonal possibilities. Twelve-tone composers in particular have used the chromatic scale to escape the restrictions of the tonal system of the related diatonic scales and keys. They evolved a variety of ways to arrange all twelve tones of the chromatic scale in a linear *twelve-tone row* that could serve as the basic interval structure for the melodic, harmonic, and structural organization of a piece. Tonality as an organizing principle was abandoned.

Luigi Dallapiccola organized the tones of the chromatic scale (Example 10-9) into the twelve-tone row (Example 10-10) from which the melodic and harmonic material in his *Quaderno Musicale di Anna-libera* is derived.

Example 10-9.   The chromatic scale

Example 10-10.   Twelve-tone row utilized by **Dallapiccola** in *Quaderno Musicale di Annalibera*

In Exercises 10-7 and 10-8 examine the examples in relation to the form of the twelve-tone row in Example 10-10—its numerical order of tones and its interval structure.

EXERCISE 10-7

A   Number each tone in each chord in Examples 10-11 and 10-12 that coincides with the number in the twelve-tone row.

Example 10-11.

B   List the intervals included in each chord.
C   What relationship is there between these chords, triads, and complex chords?
D   Is there a tone in each chord that could function as a root?

Example 10-12.

EXERCISE 10-8

Use Example 10-10 to construct other chords of:

    1
A   three tones: 2 etc.
    3

    1
B   four tones: 2 etc.
    3
    4

Construct the chords in closed position; open position; and both open and closed position, moving from one to the other. (Transpose tones up or down when necessary for good voice leading.)

Twelve-Tone Mirror Formations   A twelve-tone row can be transposed to any pitch level, and it can be inverted. Chords can be constructed that use the inverted form of the row to "mirror" the original chords.

EXERCISE 10-9

A   Using the original twelve-tone row in Example 10-10 as a guide, write an inversion of the original row, starting on a♯.
B   transpose the original row up an augmented fourth (e′).

C   invert the transposed row.

D   Using your inversion of the original twelve-tone row as a guide, write the mirror versions (inversions) of the chords constructed in Exercise 10-8.

Tonal Mirror Formations   Chords can be constructed on any tone of the ascending diatonic scale, and its descending inverted form, so as to mirror the original scale and chords.

EXERCISE 10-10

A   List the intervals included in the original chords of Example 10-13, as well as the intervals included in their mirror version.

Example 10-13.   **Bartók:** *Mikrokosmos*, Vol. 4, No. 120

B   Is Example 10-13 an *exact* mirror—that is, a version in which the interval structure of the original is maintained in its mirror form, as in Exercise 10-9D? If not, where are the differences?

C   On what scale is this mirror image based?

RESULTS   There are two forms of mirror inversions. In one, the interval structure of the original is precisely duplicated in mirror form; an *exact* mirror image is produced (see Exercise 10-9D). In the other, the interval structure of the mirror image is confined to a specific key and the tones of the scale of the key; a *tonal* mirror image is produced (see Exercise 10-10).

EXERCISE 10-11

A   Write a tonal mirror version of Exercise 8-4A, starting on c′ and using *only* tones of the C major scale.

B   Write an exact mirror version of Exercise 8-4A, starting on c′ and using accidentals (♯, ♭) when necessary.

To Sum Up   The more new tones added to any chord, the more complex its interval structure, the more dissonant its character, and the more ambiguous its root.

Besides the intervallic structure of a chord, the factors of dynamics, register, instrumentation, and musical context will affect the chord's consonant/dissonant quality and help determine its most likely root, if any.

Any extended chord reduced within an octave will become more complicated in structure and more concentrated in its sound mass. Multi-tone chords create a thicker texture and a greater sense of musical space.

The most dense sound mass (that uses pitch) is the tone cluster. The texture of a tone cluster is so thick that musical space can seem "crowded."

PROJECT 10-1

Using Exercises 10-7–10-9 to construct additional three- and four-tone chords that incorporate *other* combinations of tones $\begin{matrix} 1 & 2 \\ 3 & 4 \\ 5 & 6 \end{matrix}$ etc.

$\begin{matrix} 1 & 2 \\ 4 & 5 \\ 7 & 8 \\ 10 & 11 \end{matrix}$ etc., and using mirror forms of the various chords in various positions, registers, and dynamics, create a dramatic piece for piano and/or woodwinds. You can combine chords (original and mirror version) to create *sound masses* that contrast in texture with three-tone chords, intervals, or single tones.

PROJECT 10-1
(VARIATIONS)

1 Proceed as above, but intersperse triads and extended triads that act as "chords of resolution" to twelve-tone dissonant chord combinations.

2 Proceed as in variation 1, but use triads and extended triads in the middle register for voices, and use smooth voice leading. The piano and/or winds can be used throughout their range, as in Project 10-1. The voices should act as a textural counterpoint to the instrumental part(s). Use vocal sounds (vowels and consonants) or words as part of the vocal sonority.

PROJECT 10-2

Using a folk melody or a Bach chorale, write a piece for voice and piano. Harmonize the piece with tense chords in which the tones of the melody conflict with the tones of the harmony.

PROJECT 10-3

Write a short, tonal piano piece in C major (white keys), using chords and their mirror image. (The two forms of the chord need not coincide.)

LISTENING
SUGGESTIONS

Berg: Violin Concerto, first movement
Ravel: *Daphnis and Chloe:* Suite No. 2

Observe the types of chords and the way each composer uses them. Describe. Does each approach produce a different "atmosphere"?

Ives: "Majority," from *114 Songs*

Observe the use of tone clusters.

BIBLIOGRAPHY: SECTION II

Brindle, Reginald S., *Serial Composition.* London, New York: Oxford University Press, 1966.

Helmholtz, Hermann von, *On the Sensations of Tone as a Physiological Basis for the Theory of Music.* New York: P. Smith, 1948.

Hindemith, Paul, *A Composer's World.* Cambridge, Mass.: Harvard University Press, 1952.

Hindemith, Paul, *The Craft of Musical Composition,* Book II. New York: Associated Music Publishers, 1945.

Leibowitz, Rene, *Schoenberg and His School.* New York: Da Capo, 1970.

Persichetti, Vincent, *Twentieth Century Harmony.* New York: Norton, 1961.

Salzer, Felix, *Structural Hearing.* New York: Charles Boni, 1952.

Sessions, Roger, *The Musical Experience of Composer, Performer, Listener.* Princeton, N.J.: Princeton University Press, 1958.

3 *Time*

GENERAL OBJECTIVE

To *develop* an awareness of the clock time in which music moves and the musical time that is created through rhythm, tempo, and meter.

11 BASIC NOTIONS OF TIME

OBJECTIVE

To *study* the relationship between rhythm, tempo, and meter.

CAPSULE DEFINITIONS

Clock time	Chronological time.
Felt time	Subjective (or psychological) time.
Musical time	Musical "idea" unfolding through tempo, rhythm, and meter to create musical "form."
Rhythmic pattern	A grouping of tones organized in a time pattern.
Rhythm	Larger flows of sound through time.
Tempo	Speed of beats (slow, fast, etc.).
Meter	Small flow of time composed of recurring beats grouped into measures separated by bar lines.
Phrase unit	A grouping of tones within a phrase.
Phrase	A cohesive part of a music idea, usually two to four measures long, articulated by a cadence.
Cadence	Harmonic and/or melodic "breathing" point at the end of a phrase.

Music requires sound, space, and time. We know that sound moves through *real space*. As it does, it creates *musical space* through tones, intervals, chords, and high and low nonpitched sounds. We know that sound takes time to travel. We *see* the baseball bat hit the ball, but we *hear* the sound seconds later. We also know that a sound has duration and that this duration can be measured. Sound extends into both space and time.

Time is usually thought of as something we *measure*. The duration of an action is measured in milliseconds, seconds, minutes, and hours. These smaller units of time help us to order our everyday lives, and musical events as well, into meaningful and coherent patterns.

In music, time is perceived as the unfolding of musical events or ideas through large and small rhythmic flow patterns. These rhythmic patterns are organized into smaller units of time that are divided into "measures." A system of *meters* ($\frac{3}{4}$, $\frac{5}{8}$, etc.) determines the number of beats that are to be grouped into a measure. A proportional system of note values (o, ♩, ♩ etc.) determines the duration of each *note value* or the number of beats each note value is to receive (o = ♩ ♩, ♩ = ♩ ♩). A system of *tempos* (slow, fast, etc.) regulates the speed of these note values and the flow of music.

Time is also thought of as ongoing—with a past, present, and future. It "flows" on. Its "passing" lets us look back, as well as project ahead. These larger flows of time help us to organize our lives into longer-range patterns. These patterns can be measured in hours, days, months, and years, and they deal with larger life-rhythms: the school year, summer vacation, the seasons, the natural cycles of day and night— other levels of real time. In a somewhat similar way, a musical idea, gesture, or phrase involves a larger time frame.

Each coherent rhythmic pattern—which is stated through a group of tones, a motive, or a phrase unit in a particular meter and tempo— combines, forming larger rhythmic groupings of measures, phrases, periods, sections, and movements in the same or related meters and tempos to expand the time frame in which the music unfolds. We perceive the larger rhythmic groupings as an entity—a "musical idea."

The elaboration of the musical idea in clock time through meter and tempo is *felt* to have a particular sense of time both in speed and duration. A slow movement (adagio) may not actually last longer than a fast one (allegro), but may *seem* longer. When listening to music or seeing a play or film, have you ever been surprised by the discrepancy between your sense of time and the actual clock time of the experience?

EXERCISE 11-1

A   Snap your fingers once. Snap your fingers again when you think five seconds have passed.

B   Repeat A. This time, use your watch to determine when you should snap your fingers for the second time.

C   Make various soft, slow, irregular sounds for five seconds.

D   Repeat C as one of your classmates plays musical fragments at various points during the five-second period.

QUESTIONS AND
OBSERVATIONS

1   Do A and B seem equal in duration? If not, which one seems longer? Why?

2   Do B and C seem equal in duration? If not, which one seems longer? Why? (If you are not sure, repeat the exercise.)

3   How long did the silence in A actually last?

RESULTS

B and C lasted the same amount of time. But our *perception* of the time each event lasted could be different.

How long we think an action lasted often doesn't match with the facts.

Some events affect us directly. Others may *eventually* affect us, even though we aren't directly involved in them. A sense of closeness to a highly charged or recurring event makes time *appear* to pass quickly (Exercise 11-1D). But when events either seem too distant to affect us or occur infrequently, time appears to pass slowly (Exercise 11-1B). Clock time then appears to be inconsistent with our perception of time. Since clock time is constant, we should talk about two levels of time: (1) *clock time* and (2) *felt time,* in which we perceive time as moving either quickly or slowly.

We could say that we live our lives at various time levels simultaneously, phasing in and out from clock time to felt time. We invest clock time with significance, transforming it to felt time.

There are similarities between subjective felt time and musical time. In Exercise 11-2, Examples 11-1 and 11-2 take approximately five seconds each.

EXERCISE 11-2

A   Play Examples 11-1 and 11-2.

Example 11-1.   **Beethoven:** *Symphony No. 5*, fourth movement

Allegro (♩ = 84)

etc.

Example 11-2.   **Debussy:** *Nocturnes:* "Nuages"

Modiré

B   Repeat Exercise 11-1.

QUESTIONS AND
OBSERVATIONS
Did Examples 11-1 and 11-2 seem equal in duration? If not, which seemed longer? Why?

Exercises 11-1 and 11-2 each took approximately five seconds. However, our perception of the time each took could be different. Slower-moving, infrequent musical events, like real events can appear to take longer than recurring and faster-moving musical events.

Our perception of time is subjective, and affects the way we react to real and musical events.

But in music, sound events, which exist as part of a language, are more abstract than real events. A sound involves us immediately: we expect it to continue combining with other related sounds. Although clock time is required for the sound to evolve into a musical idea, the first sound, like a thought, creates its own *time*—and motion.

As musical time is created, sounds combine with other sounds in a specific tempo and meter and form into musical ideas with larger rhythmic time flows. The various levels of space and time combine into a cohesive whole that is greater than any of its parts. The combination and synthesis of various time levels is perceived a musical time.

EXERCISE 11-3

A   Play Examples 11-1 and 11-2.
B   Repeat A while one of your classmates makes an arc (⟶) with his arm from the beginning to the end of each "idea."
C   Repeat A, but accent each measure in Example 11-1 and each beat in Example 11-2.
D   Repeat C while one or more of your classmates finger-snaps each accent.

QUESTIONS AND
OBSERVATIONS

1   In which version(s) of the two examples did you have a sense of the "whole idea" as one time unit from the beginning to the end?

2   In which version(s) was the "idea" fragmented into more than one time unit? Why?

3   Was your perception of time different in each case?

4   Did the accents in C and the finger-snaps in D affect your perception of time?

Our perception of time (felt time) in Examples 11-1 and 11-2, which depended on the tempo, the closeness, and the recurrence of sounds, could be different. But our perception of musical time was drastically altered when the meter in Example 11-1 and the beat in Example 11-2 were accented. This accentuation fragmented the rhythmic time flow of the whole musical idea into various smaller, even-flowing units of time. This reduced the effect of the time levels of tempo and rhythm, the harmonic rhythm, and the motivic rhythm on the flow of the phrase.

The same distortion of our perception of musical time would occur if we imposed a meter on music that was conceived rhythmically, such as Gregorian chant. The distortion of one time level at the expense of other time levels can inhibit our perception of musical time.

To Sum Up   *Musical time* is born with sound and its perception. It requires, first, the "musical idea," which can exist on various spatial and temporal levels. It then requires someone to perceive the temporal/spatial musical events that register as the musical idea. With the perception of the musical idea, *real time* becomes transformed to *musical time*.

Music is an abstract language whose associations are physical (residing in the properties of the sound) and historical (residing in the arrangement of sound in specific ways by particular cultures). Its expectations are caused by the sound and its arrangement. The first sound or group of sounds (the musical idea) is experienced along with the expectation of its completion. The musical idea, with its unfolding in clock time through the various levels of time, creates musical time.

These various time levels include tempo, rhythm, meter, and duration. They are expressed through motives, melody, harmony, and texture. The combination of these time levels produces a time entity greater than any of its parts, which is identified as *musical time*. Form is created in the unfolding of the musical idea, from its inception to its completion. The apprehension of this unfolding through musical form is the apprehension of musical time.

12 TIME: Rhythm

OBJECTIVE

To *study* the relationship between rhythm as a "flow of time" and the musical "idea" (motive or line), harmony, and phrase.

CAPSULE DEFINITIONS

Rhythmic motive	A short identifiable rhythmic pattern that appears in a melodic motive and/or in an accompaniment motive.
Phrase unit	A cohesive grouping of tones within a phrase. (Two phrase units could constitute a phrase.)
Phrase	A cohesive musical idea or portion of a melody; sometimes four measures in length.
Period	A part or whole of a larger music idea ordinarily consisting of two complementary phrases.
Sections	A larger part of a musical structure consisting of no less than one period, and ordinarily many periods.
Movement	A complete part of a large, many-movement work.
Shape-form	The music as it evolves structurally.

A. Preliminary Explorations

In the music of the thirteenth through the seventeenth centuries, rhythm meant "the flow" or "flowing meter" of mensural notation (the temporal relationships between note values).

Rhythm exists in the cycles of the seasons, the earth's rotation, the cycle of life and death, the arc of a cathedral, the artist's brush stroke, a musical phrase, and the gesture of a person's walk, an athlete's jump, and a ballerina's leap. In each, there is a coherent and identifiable flow of energy, time, and intent from inception to completion. These patterns are repeatable, variable, and measurable.

Although each rhythmic flow of energy/time/intent is indivisible when it is seen or felt as a coherent pattern, it contains subdivisions of energy/time/intent that can be measured. The whole is the sum of its parts: the rhythmic flow pattern consists of rhythmic motives and metrical beat patterns.

EXERCISE 12-1

A   Make an arc (⌒➤) with your right arm for five seconds. At the completion of the motion, repeat it with your left arm for the same amount of time. (Repeat a few times without any interruption of the flow.)

B   Snap your fingers five times, one per second (♩ = 60) with the right hand. (Keep the right hand in the same snapping position.)

C   Repeat B, but move your left hand forward and then backward, each gesture taking five seconds.

D   Repeat B, but move your left hand forward for three seconds and backward for two seconds.

E   Repeat B, but move your left hand forward for four seconds and backward for three seconds.

F   Repeat B, but move your left hand forward and backward without synchronizing its gesture with the right hand's snap.

G   Make an arc with your left arm for five seconds while you snap your fingers with your right arm, one snap per second (♩ = 60).

H   Repeat G, but slow down each snap. Your arc should be completed before you complete your five snaps.

I   Snap once, and follow with five seconds of silence. (Repeat a few times.)

J   Snap indiscriminately, interspersing the snaps with silence.

133

1   In which exercises did you feel a rhythmic flow of time?
2   In which exercises did you feel a rhythmic flow of time that was sup-
    ported by another unit of time?
3   In which exercise(s) did you feel a rhythmic flow of time that was
    contradicted by another unit of time?
4   In which exercise(s) did you feel two rhythmic flows of time? How can
    these be considered as parts of an even larger rhythmic flow of time?
    Describe.
5   In which exercise(s) did you feel no flow of time?

It is apparent that two or more time levels can coexist, whether
they are related or unrelated. Those that relate will support the larger
time flow. The metric finger-snaps will support the motion of the
rhythmic arc. The irregular finger snaps in H and J and the motions in
F that are not synchronized at any point do not make a coherent pattern
and therefore will not support the motion of the arc. The two time levels
in H and J contradict each other; thus, no coherent rhythmic patterns
are established there.

B. Rhythmic Motives

Although we talk of a rhythmic flow as indivisible, it is clear from
Example 12-1 that this flow encompasses a small subdivision of energy/
time/intent called a *rhythmic motive*. The rhythmic motive is related to
the larger rhythmic flow pattern as a melodic motive is related to the
melody.

Beethoven's Symphony No. 5 begins with a motive that is both
melodic and rhythmic. This motive is based on the interval of a third
and a group of repeated eighth notes (Example 12-1).

Example 12-1.   **Beethoven:** *Symphony No. 5*, beginning

It is a cohesive and independent unit that combines and contributes to
the larger melodic-rhythmic flow pattern.

In Exercise 12-1, D and E, the forward and backward motions of the left hand (whether these motions took the same or a different amount of time) became absorbed by the larger repeated rhythmic pattern in the same way that the motive became absorbed by the larger rhythmic flow pattern in the Beethoven symphony.

EXERCISE 12-2

Examples 12-2–12-6 contain both larger melodic-rhythmic flow patterns (phrases) and smaller melodic-rhythmic patterns (motives).

Example 12-2.   "Benedicamus Domino" (plainsong)

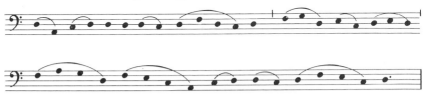

Example 12-3.   Crumb: *Voices of Ancient Children*

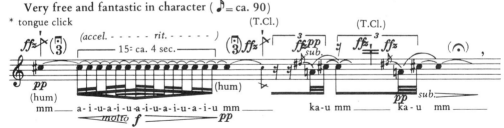

Example 12-4.   Schubert: *Symphony No. 8,* first movement

Example 12-5.   Stravinsky: *The Firebird:* "Dance of the Princess"

Example 12-6.   **J. S. Bach:** *Brandenberg Concerto No. 3,* first movement

A Mark the phrase units in each example.

B Mark the motivic units within each example.

C Observe the interval structure of the melody and the harmony.

D Describe the tensions created harmonically, melodically, and rhythmically within the phrase.

E How do these tensions and their resolutions help the movement of the melodic-rhythmic flow?

In each of these examples, there is a continuation of the musical idea through related melodic-rhythmic flow patterns that form into complementary phrases, periods, sections, movements, and, finally, entire pieces.

C. Harmonic Rhythm

In addition to the melodic-rhythmic flow patterns, there is a related harmonic-rhythmic flow pattern.

EXERCISE 12-3

A Mark the change of chords in Examples 12-4 and 12-6.

B What is the duration of each chord?

C What is the relationship of the changes of harmony to the melodic-rhythmic flow?

RESULTS   The harmony, in addition to supporting the melody, has its own "rhythm." The duration of each chord is usually longer than the duration of the tones of the melody. The harmonic rhythm therefore appears to move more slowly than the melodic rhythm. Harmonic rhythm represents another "slower-moving" rhythmic time level.

To Sum Up   Rhythm refers to the larger musical flow patterns, which are identifiable as coherent flows of energy, time, and intent. These flow patterns are perceived through short, melodic, rhythmic, motives: a melodic-rhythmic line or a harmonic-rhythmic progression. These elements combine to form a composite musical texture and create an evolving musical shape-form consisting of phrases, periods, sections, and movements. Metrical units and their even flow of grouped "beats" act on another time level to support the rhythmic time level.

PROJECT 12-1

Take a stanza of a poem in English with *traditional* (accentual and syllabic) meter. Break it down into related rhythmic flow patterns in which an idea, thought, or feeling is carried through. Set the words "rhythmically" for voice (or use the word rhythms for percussion) so that the rhythmic flow patterns are clearly articulated musically. You could use percussion as an accompaniment (metrical background) to support the rhythmic flow of the voice (or percussion) part.

PROJECT 12-2

Take a movement of a Beethoven sonata or an Ives song. Reduce the various levels of musical activity (melodic, harmonic, etc.) to the rhythmic level, so that they lack fixed pitches. Set the "rhythm" of each part for percussion instruments.

LISTENING
SUGGESTIONS

Stravinsky: Symphony in Three Movements, second movement
J. S. Bach: Sonata for Violin and Keyboard in A Major

Note the relationship of the length of the phrases to the melodic-rhythmic line.

Beethoven: Symphony No. 5, first movement

Note how the melodic-rhythmic motive is used throughout the movement. Describe.

ANALYSIS 12-1

Examine Schubert's Symphony No. 8, first movement, and Bach's *Brandenberg Concerto No. 3*, first movement.
In each case, mark complementary phrases and describe how they relate to the original phrase (Examples 12-4 and 12-6).

13 TIME: Tempo

OBJECTIVES

1. To *study* the relationship between the *speed*, the *character*, and the *form* of a piece.

2. To *recognize* the relationship between *tempo*—the speed of the beat—and *pulse*—the pacing of the music in time.

CAPSULE DEFINITIONS

Allegro	Fast.
Adagio	Slow.
Moderato	Moderately.
Lebhaft	Moving.
Langsamer	Slower.
A Tempo	Resuming the tempo.
Wieder lebhaft	A tempo; moving again.

Basic conducting gestures:

2 2 2
4 2 8

3 3 3
4 2 8

4 4 4
4 2 8

Each piece of music has its particular sound, which is elaborated over a period of time in a variety of rhythmic flow patterns that result in a particular shape-form. Each piece has its pace: it moves at a certain speed. Robert Schumann called this pace "the movement's inner measure." Richard Wagner related tempo to good phrasing and expression. A dance, a march, and a song each expresses its character in its sound and in its tempo. If the tempo is too fast or too slow, the character of the piece is altered or destroyed.

EXERCISE 13-1

Listen to:

A Johann Strauss: "Emperor" Waltz
B Sousa: "Stars and Stripes Forever"
C Joplin: "Maple Leaf Rag"
D Billie Holiday singing "Bloody Sunday"

Describe the character of each piece. Is the tempo strictly maintained, or are there slight tempo "deviations"?

EXERCISE 13-2

Take one or two of the examples in Exercise 13-1.

A Speed up each one slightly.
B Speed up each one moderately.
C Speed up each one drastically.
D Slow up each one slightly.
E Slow up each one moderately.
F Slow up each one drastically.

QUESTIONS AND OBSERVATIONS

1 When the tempo of a piece is changed, is the piece still recognizable? What is maintained? What is lost?
2 How much can the tempo of each piece be changed before its basic character is destroyed?

Each piece appears to have a correct tempo and appears to be slightly flexible in regard to minor tempo deviations. Great tempo changes can affect the character of the piece. But if the tempo of a piece *never* deviates from beginning to end, this can also affect the character of the piece.

EXERCISE 13-3

Take any piece of music studied thus far, and follow its tempo from beginning to end. (Use a metronome or tap your finger lightly.)

1   Is the tempo strictly maintained?
2   If not, where does it deviate?
3   Does this tempo deviation serve a musical purpose? Describe.

Listen to another recording of the same piece. Compare the tempos and their effect on each interpretation of the piece.

Tempo, then, refers to the *movement* of the music and its expressive character. Tempo also refers to the *speed* of the "beat," or its rate of change. Tempo is measured by the number of recurring beats per minute.

If you walk eighty steps each minute, your walking tempo would be eighty beats per minute, which would be designated ♩ = 80 on a metronome. This designation means that there would be eighty quarter-note beats (♩) per minute.

EXERCISE 13-4

A   How many quarter notes (♩) in a minute if the tempo were designated as:

♩ = 60?

♩ = 120?

B   How many half notes (♩) in a minute if the tempo were designated as:

♩ = 60?

♩ = 120?

C   How many quarter notes (♩) in a minute if the tempo were designated as:

♩ = 60?

♩ = 120?

D   How many whole notes (o) in a minute if the tempo were designated as:

♩ = 60?

♩ = 120?

EXERCISE 13-5

A Beat ♩ =80 with your right arm in the following manner:

etc.

B Increase the tempo gradually from ♩ = 80 to ♩ = 160.

C Decrease the tempo gradually from ♩ = 80 to ♩ = 40.

D Beat ♩ = 160, alternating a strong beat with a weak beat:

etc.

E Beat ♩ = 40, alternating a strong first half of the beat with a weak *afterbeat*, or second half of the beat:

etc.

QUESTIONS AND
OBSERVATIONS

1 Does one tempo seem more comfortable to beat and feel than another? Which one?

2 Describe your reactions to A and D, and then to A and E. What does each pair have in common? Does the second beat in D feel like a beat? Does the afterbeat in E feel like a beat?

3 Describe your reactions to B and C.

Compare your responses in Exercise 13-5 with those in Exercise 13-2.

It should be clear that the beat as a basic pulse must be maintained in the same tempo, or the character of the piece is altered. A tempo that is very fast or very slow seems to have two levels of beats. In Exercise 13-5E (♩ = 40), the quarter-note beats move so slowly that there is another level of beats—quicker-moving eighth-note beats (♪ = 80). In Exercise 13-5D (♩ = 160), the quarter-note beats move so quickly that there is also a level of slower-moving half-note beats (♩ = 80). There is a "pairing" of beats in Exercise 13-5D and a pairing of beat and after beat in Exercise 13-5E. Although the tempos in these two exercises have a different beat speed, both have the same pulse speed (or rate) of eighty pulses (︵) per minute.

In ♩ = 40, there are two pulses per beat:

In ♩ = 160, there are two beats per pulse:

In $\quad \downarrow = 80$, pulse is coincident with beat:

Although the *tempo* of a piece is tied to the speed of the beat and the *character* of a piece is tied to the beat itself, the *pulse* is felt as the underlying "heartbeat" of the piece. It is the pulse that relates movement to movement and piece to piece. The pulse rate can change as it adjusts to the changes in tempo.

Repeat Exercise 13-5, B and C. Start with a beat and pulse that coincide. At what point do you experience a "pairing of the beats" and a readjustment of the pulse?

In the three preceding examples, the relation of pulse to beat was 2 to 1, 1 to 2, and 1 to 1. In pieces whose tempo is very fast, there may be one pulse to every three beats.

EXERCISE 13-6

How would you beat Examples 13-1 and 13-2?

Example 13-1.   **Beethoven:** *Symphony No. 9*, scherzo, mm. 177–83

Example 13-2.   **Beethoven:** *Symphony No. 9*, scherzo, mm. 234–40

RESULTS   Each measure would receive one stroke (↓). For a conductor, however, each stroke (↓) would indicate a *down-beat* to the orchestra. Does each measure have a down-beat feeling? If not, which measures do? As a conductor, then, you must be able to group various beats together to form a measure, or (in this case) a phrase. Example 13-1 could be conducted as a three-pattern (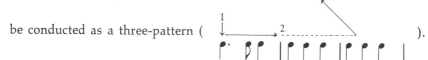).

Each measure would equal a beat, and three measures (three beats) would equal the phrase and the pulse. Example 13-2 could be conducted

as a four pattern (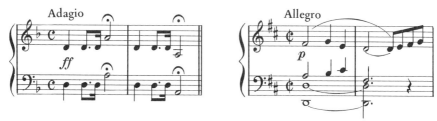) in which measures one

and two and measures three and four equal two pulses and one phrase.

In many pieces, there are changes of tempo indicated in the score. A classical symphony may begin with an adagio introduction followed by an allegro section (Example 13-3).

Example 13-3.   Haydn: *Symphony No. 104,* first movement

Although the character and beat of the adagio are quite different from those of the allegro, there is a relationship between the two sections, one in which the *pulse* is the cohesive force.

On the other hand, a change of tempo may alter the underlying pulse (Example 13-4).

Example 13-4.   Webern: *Variations for Orchestra*

In both pieces the change of tempo, besides signaling a change of character, helps to articulate the evolving shape-form. In Example 13-4, the change of tempo also helps to articulate phrase structure, functioning as a cadential harmony in a classical piece.

Many twentieth-century composers have used contrasting tempos simultaneously, as, for instance, in Example 13-5.

Example 13-5.

Different tempos (whether employed simultaneously or successively) represent different time levels—some with the same underlying pulse, others with more than one pulse. In Exercise 13-7, two contrasting tempos are superimposed. Listen for the relationship between beat and pulse.

EXERCISE 13-7

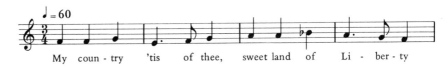

My coun - try   'tis   of thee,   sweet land   of   Li - ber - ty

    A   Sing while one or more of your classmates snaps their fingers at the tempo, ♩ = 80.

    B   Repeat, reversing the roles.

EXERCISE 13-8

Sing while one or more of your classmates snaps their fingers at the tempo, ♩ = 120 and one or more classmates brushes one hand against the other, like cymbals, at the tempo, ♩ = 60.

RESULTS   In Exercise 13-7, there are two different simultaneous tempos and pulse rates (⟶). These tempos and pulse rates coincide every measure

$$\left(\begin{array}{l} \rightarrow \ \ \Box = 60 \ (\Box\Box\Box) \\ \rightarrow \ \ \Box = 80 \ (\Box\Box\Box\Box) \end{array} \right)$$

to form a third, slower-moving tempo

♩. = 20

o = 20

$$(\ \ \left. \begin{array}{l} \Box. \\ \mathrm{o} \end{array} \right\} = 20 \ ).$$

In Exercise 13-8, there are three different simultaneous tempos but two different pulse rates ($\rightarrow$). These coincide every measure

$$\begin{array}{ll}
\text{♩} = 30 & \\
\rightarrow \text{♩} = 60 & (\text{♩♩}) \\
\quad\text{♪} = 120 & (\text{♪♪♪♪}) \\
\rightarrow \text{♪} = 90 & (\text{♪♪♪}) \\
\quad\text{♩.} = 30 & \\
\left(\begin{array}{l} \text{♩} \\ \text{♩.} \end{array} \right\} = 30 \quad)
\end{array}$$

to form a third, slower-moving tempo

To Sum Up

Tempo defines the *character* of a piece of music in relation to its *movement* or pace. Specifically, it refers to the rate of speed from beat to beat.

In a moderate tempo, beat can be synonomous with pulse. In a very fast tempo, beats form into groups of two or three per pulse. In a very slow tempo, the beat divides into two or three pulses per beat. Pulse and beats represent two time levels that are directly related to each other (in the ratio of 1 to 1, 2 to 1, 1 to 2, or 1 to 3, or 3 to 1). In pieces that contain two or more simultaneous or successive tempos, there are multiple time levels.

Tempo and tempo changes can help to articulate phrase structure and the evolving shape-form.

PROJECT 13-1

Take at least three projects that you have already completed. Carefully edit each with correct tempo marks, dynamics, and instrumental articulations, and revise when necessary.

PROJECT 13-2

Write three short character pieces—for one, two, and three *different* instruments. Each should be based upon minimal musical material and careful use of tempo.

PROJECT 13-3

Write a piece that uses two or more tempos successively and/or simultaneously to create various related tempo levels and to help articulate the phrase structure.

Webern: Variations for Orchestra
Ives: *Three Places in New England,* second movement
Beethoven: String Quartet, Op. 132, first and second movements

Note how each composer uses tempo. Describe the beat-pulse relationships in each tempo and the relationship of one tempo to another.

14 *TIME:* Meter

OBJECTIVES

1. To *study* the various meters used in music.
2. To *learn* to notate meter—note values and time signature.

CAPSULE DEFINITIONS

Meter	Groupings of two, three, or more recurring beats.
Types of meter	*simple meter:* duple (binary): $\frac{2}{4}$ $\frac{2}{2}$ $\frac{2}{8}$
	triple (ternary): $\frac{3}{4}$ $\frac{3}{2}$ $\frac{3}{8}$
	compound meter: $\frac{4}{4}$ $\frac{4}{2}$ $\frac{4}{8}$, $\frac{5}{4}$ $\frac{5}{2}$ $\frac{5}{8}$, $\frac{6}{4}$ etc.
	polymeter: more than one meter at same time: $\frac{2}{4}$ etc. $\frac{3}{8}$
Time signature	Indicates the number of beats ($\frac{2}{4}$ etc.) grouped in a measure.
Measure; bar	One grouping of beats bound by a bar line.
Slur	Connects various notes in the same "breath."

A. Preliminary Explorations

Rhythm is the extended flow of time, energy, and intent. *Tempo* measures the pace of that time flow as it regulates the speed of beats. *Meter* groups those beats together in regularly recurring time patterns bound by measures and bar lines and indicated by the *time signature*— $\frac{4}{4}$, $\frac{3}{4}$, $\frac{6}{8}$, and so on. Even recurring beats tend to group themselves in units of two or three.

EXERCISE 14-1

       A   Play/listen Examples 14-1–14-3.

Example 14-1.   **Foster:** *"Oh! Susanna"*

Example 14-2.   **Beethoven:** *String Quartet, Op. 131*, scherzo

Example 14-3.   **Beethoven:** *Symphony No. 3*, first movement

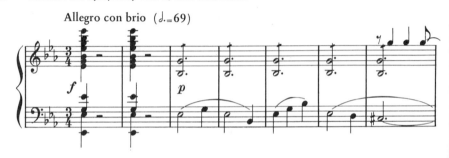

B What is the tempo of each example?
C How do the beats group themselves in each?
D What is the meter of each?
E What is the pulse of each?

RESULTS   In Example 14-1 ($\frac{2}{4}$ time), beats group themselves in units of two per measure. In Example 14-2 ($\frac{2}{2}$ or cut time), beats also group themselves in units of two per measure. Since the tempo is fast (as in most of Beethoven's scherzos) however, the normal grouping of two beats is felt as one beat. In Example 14-3 ($\frac{3}{4}$ time), beats group themselves in units of three per measure. But because of the fast tempo of each example, each contains only one pulse per measure.

B. Notation of Simple Meter: Time Signatures and Note Values

Specific pitch can be measured and notated. The various flows of time, including tempo and meter, can also be measured and notated. Speed rates are specified by various tempo designations that range from slow (such as adagio) to fast (such as allegro). In addition, more precise metronome markings can be used, as in Example 14-3, where ♩. = 69 means that each ♩. is somewhat faster than a second or that 69 ♩. equal one minute.

In a simple *duple* (or *binary*) meter ($\frac{2}{4}$), the beats are grouped two $\left(\frac{②}{4}\right)$ per measure, a quarter note $\left(\frac{2}{④}\right)$ equal to a beat. In a simple *triple* (or *ternary* meter $\frac{③}{4}$), the beats are grouped three $\left(\frac{③}{4}\right)$ per measure, a quarter note $\left(\frac{3}{④}\right)$ equal to a beat.

In each of these simple meters (which are indicated by a time signature), beats can be arranged in various ways. However, a measure can *only* include combinations of beats that add up to the number of beats indicated in the time signature.

Simple meters include other duple and triple beat groupings.

EXERCISE 14-2

A List the musical examples in $\frac{2}{4}$ and in $\frac{3}{4}$ from the previous chapters.

B How many beats per measure in each of the following?

$\frac{3}{8}$ $\frac{2}{2}$ ¢ $\frac{3}{2}$ $\frac{2}{8}$ $\frac{2}{16}$ $\frac{3}{16}$

C   What note value would equal a *beat* in A? in B?

D   Tap out (or conduct) each meter in A and B, accenting each down-
beat in various tempos—slow, moderate, and fast.

The beat can be divided into two, three, four, or more equal note
values. These include:

1   duplets of:
   two eighth notes: ♪ ♪ = ♫ =(♩)

   two sixteenth notes: ♪ ♪ = ♬ =(♪)

2   triplets of:
   three quarter notes: ♩ ♩ ♩ =(♩.)

   three eighth notes: ♫♪ =(♩)

   three sixteenth notes: ♬ =(♪)

3   quadruplets of:
   four sixteenth notes: ♬ =(♩)

Subdivisions of each of these are also possible.

Beats are not limited to simple divisions of two, three, and four.
Divisions of five and seven though somewhat less frequent, are possible
(♬♪ , ♬♬). Beat divisions of five and seven often
occur in songs, where they accommodate several syllables that occur on
one beat in a free-flowing speechlike style. Divisions of six can be in-
terpreted in two possible ways:

two groups of three: ♬♬ =(♫ = ♩)

three groups of two: ♬♬ =(♬ = ♩)

A beat can also be *combined* with other beats to form larger note
values (Example 14-4).

Example 14-4.   Combined beats

$$\text{♩} + \text{♩} = \text{♩}\qquad\qquad \text{♩} + \text{♩} = \text{o}$$

Note that placing a *dot* after a note increases the value of the note by one half.

EXERCISE 14-3

Write two four-measure "rhythmic" exercises for percussion that incorporate two different meters from Exercise 14-2. Use various note values that equal the correct number of beats per measure indicated in the time signature. For example:

Just as various beats can be combined into larger note values, various *parts* of the beat can be combined. In a meter where a quarter note equals a beat (for example, $\frac{2}{4}$ or $\frac{3}{4}$), the divisions of the beat would include the note values in Example 14-5.

Example 14-5.   Combined parts

In a meter where an eighth note equals a beat (for instance, $\frac{2}{8}$ or $\frac{3}{8}$), each of the comparable note values of Examples 14-1 and 14-2 would be halved. In a meter where a half note equals a beat (such as $\frac{2}{2}$ or $\frac{3}{2}$), each of the comparable note values of Examples 14-1 and 14-2 would be doubled.

Other note values occur when the beat is combined with smaller note values. In a meter where a quarter note equals a beat (such as $\frac{2}{4}$, $\frac{3}{4}$, or $\frac{3}{4}$) the combinations of note values in Example 14-6 would be possible.

Example 14-6.   Combined notes

EXERCISE 14-4

Write an eight-bar "rhythmic" exercise for percussion. Combine various note values that you wrote in Exercise 14-3 with those in Example 14-5. You can use slurs (⌒) to create longer note values. *Then* rewrite these note values in a clearer notation. (For example, in $\frac{3}{4}$ meter, ♩ ♫ ♬ should be rewritten as ♩. ♪♩♪ .)

To Sum Up   Each measure contains a specific number of beats. This number depends on the time signature. Although each meter has its beat pattern, these patterns can be compounded (added or divided) in various ways. Because of its position in the measure, the down-beat (or first beat) is considered the strong beat; the remainder of the beats are considered weak.

C. Notation of Rests

The composer John Cage asks, "Is there such a thing as silence? Is there always something to hear . . . ?"[1] Silence does not have any

"specific frequency" but it does act as a textural element complementary

[1] Cage, *Silence,* p. 42.

to sound. Each "sound" duration with its measured note value has a comparable "silence" duration, measured in the form of *rests*. Example 14-7 illustrates how rests are expressed in notation.

Example 14-7.   Rests in notation

$$\circ = \text{—}, \quad \raisebox{0pt}{\text{♩}} = \text{–}, \quad \raisebox{0pt}{\text{♩}} = \raisebox{0pt}{\text{𝄽}}, \quad \raisebox{0pt}{\text{♪}} = \raisebox{0pt}{\text{𝄾}}, \quad \raisebox{0pt}{\text{♫}} = \raisebox{0pt}{\text{𝄿}}$$

$$\circ\cdot = \text{—}\cdot, \quad \raisebox{0pt}{\text{♩}}\cdot = \text{–}\cdot, \quad \raisebox{0pt}{\text{♩}}\cdot = \raisebox{0pt}{\text{𝄽}}\cdot, \quad \raisebox{0pt}{\text{♪}}\cdot = \raisebox{0pt}{\text{𝄾}}\cdot, \quad \raisebox{0pt}{\text{♫}}\cdot = \raisebox{0pt}{\text{𝄿}}\cdot$$

Any rest can be placed next to any other rest in order to lengthen it. For example, — + – = —. is equal to six beats in $\frac{\text{♩}}{4}$. As with note values, the actual number of beats each rest contains depends on the meter. A whole-note rest is equal to four ♩ beats in $\frac{4}{4}$, two ♩ beats in $\frac{2}{2}$, and eight ♪ beats in $\frac{8}{8}$.

EXERCISE 14-5

A   Rewrite Exercise 14-4, substituting comparable rests for note values.
B   Rewrite Exercise 14-4, using both note value and rests.
C   Tap or clap B.
D   Are the rests in B felt? How?
E   Conduct or tap the note values but not the rests in B.
F   Are the rests in E felt? How? Does this become an element in the musical structure? In the musical flow?

RESULTS   When a meter is established, sound and silence are "heard" as part of the metrical grouping. Sound and silence function structurally, by shaping and delineating phrases and sections. They also function dramatically, by emphasizing important events in music. In a sense, there is always something to hear.

D. Compound Meter

Meters of $\frac{4}{4}$, $\frac{4}{2}$, $\frac{4}{8}$, or $\frac{4}{16}$ are traditionally classified as *simple meters*. Since any combination of simple two- and three-beat groupings constitutes a compound grouping, all such combinations will be classified as *compound meters*.

EXERCISE 14-6

Play and examine Examples 14-8–14-14.

Example 14-8.   **J. S. Bach:** *Little Notebook for Anna Magdalena Bach,* march

Example 14-9.   **Tchaikovsky:** *Symphony No. 6,* second movement

Example 14-10.   **Stravinsky:** *The Five Fingers,* No. 4

Example 14-11.   *"Ani'Qu Ne'chawu' nani' "* (Indian ghost-dance song)

Example 14-12.   **Bartók:** *Mikrokosmos,* Vol. 6, No. 153 (two excerpts)

Example 14-13.   **Beethoven:** *Piano Sonata,* Op. 22, second movement

Example 14-14.   **Bartók:** *Mikrokosmos,* Vol. 6, No. 148

QUESTIONS AND
OBSERVATIONS

1 How would you group beats in each example?

2 What would you consider to be the strong, less strong, and weak beats?

3 Could any of the examples be written in simple meter? If so, how would you write it? Why did the composer write it this way?

4 In which examples do you feel a steady pulse?

In meters of $\frac{6}{8}$, $\frac{9}{8}$, and $\frac{12}{8}$, in which each ♪ equals one beat, there is a tendency for beats to form into symmetrical groups of three as in Example 14-15. This would also be true for those meters of 6, 9, or 12 in which the ♪ , ♩ , or 𝅗𝅥 equaled a beat. Depending on the tempo, three symmetrically grouped beats can have one pulse per measure, as do the three beats in Example 14-3.

Example 14-15.   Symmetrical beats

In meters of $\frac{4}{4}$, $\frac{5}{4}$, $\frac{7}{4}$, $\frac{8}{4}$, $\frac{9}{4}$, $\frac{10}{4}$, $\frac{11}{4}$, etc., in which each ♩ gets one beat (or in the equivalent meters in which ♪ or 𝅗𝅥 equal a beat), those beats that can do so tend to form into symmetrical groups of two ($\frac{4}{4}$, $\frac{8}{4}$) or three ($\frac{9}{4}$). But most meters group in various combinations of two and/or three. The $\frac{8}{4}$ and the $\frac{9}{4}$, which *could* contain symmetrical groupings, do not always do so (see Examples 14-12 and 14-14). Depending on the tempo, symmetrically grouped beats can have one pulse. The unevenness of the *irregular* beat groupings tends to create a rhythmic tension not always present in *regular* beat groupings.

Each of the interpretations in Example 14-16 of what is strongest (∠), strong (–), and weak (⌣) is possible.

Example 14-16.   Irregular beats

EXERCISE 14-7

A Using $\frac{7}{8}$ and $\frac{4}{4}$, write two "character" dances of four to eight measures each for two percussionlike "instruments" (clapping, tapping, etc.).

B Play the two dances, observing the difference between the symmetrical and asymmetrical meters.

We could reduce each compound meter in Examples 14-11 and 14-12 and write them, as Stravinsky does in his Symphonies of Winds, (see Example 15-14) as $\frac{2}{8}$, $\frac{3}{8}$, or $\frac{2}{8}$ instead of as $\frac{7}{8}$. In spite of the asymmetry of many compound meters, "regularity" is established with the repetition of these patterns. In the Symphonies of Winds, Stravinsky obviously does not wish to regularize the pattern.

E. Conducting Simple and Compound Beat Patterns

Every student of music should have some *physical* familiarity with the time levels in music. One should be able to *feel* beats, patterns of beats, pulse, and the larger phrase flow in one's arm and one's body. These time levels are "choreographed" in conducting motions that encompass the elements of tempo, rhythm, and meter. The basic gestures reduce to the three in Examples 14-17–14-19.

Example 14-17. $\frac{2}{4}$ or equivalent

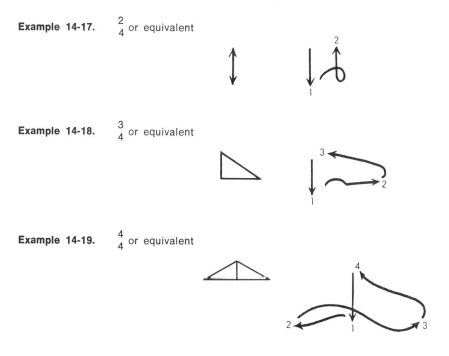

Example 14-18. $\frac{3}{4}$ or equivalent

Example 14-19. $\frac{4}{4}$ or equivalent

The $\frac{4}{4}$ or equivalent combines $\frac{3}{4}$ with a leftward gesture on beat 2. Other gestures are variants of Examples 14-20–14-22.

Example 14-20.   6/8

Example 14-21.   5/8

Example 14-22.   9/8

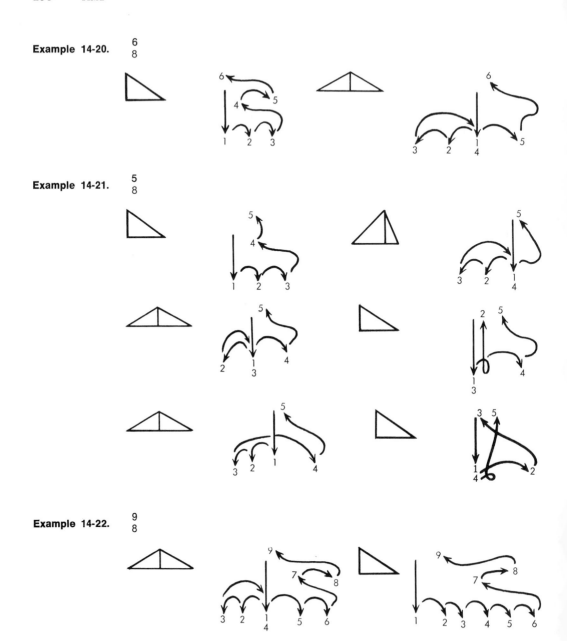

The choice of conducting gesture depends on many factors, such as tempo, meter, dynamics, instrumentation, phrase flow, and articulation. Compound meters such as $\frac{5}{8}$ $\frac{6}{8}$ and $\frac{7}{8}$ $\frac{8}{8}$ $\frac{9}{8}$ can be conducted in combinations of the basic two-, three-, and four-patterns.

EXERCISE 14-8

Conduct various examples in Chapters 13 and 14. Observe the meter and the tempo in order to determine the correct gesture.

QUESTIONS AND
OBSERVATIONS

1   In each case, describe your gesture in relation to the music.

2   Did you indicate the correct tempo and meter?

3   Did your arm "play" the music in addition to indicating the correct tempo and meter?

4   Could you conduct so that more of the music would show in your gesture? Describe what you would have to do. Try it. Did it work? Describe the difference.

By conducting, you begin to acquire a physical sense of the music and its various time levels. An instrumentalist is in touch (physical contact) with the sound level as well as the time level. The conductor is not in contact with the instrument making the sound; he is in physical contact only with the time level of the music. But his gesture must indicate more than the time level. It should also encompass the sound level, which includes texture, melodic and harmonic motion, instrumental quality, and intensity.

F. Polymeters

There are composers in the twentieth century who have used more than one meter at the same time. This technique is called *polymeter*. Polymeters can be related closely so that they converge often, or more distantly so that they converge less often.

The simplest and most related meters share either a beat, a pulse, or a smaller division of the beat. For example, the meters $\frac{6}{8}$ and $\frac{3}{4}$, in both of which the eighth note (♪) appears, would converge each measure:

The meters $\frac{6}{8}$ and $\frac{2}{4}$, in both of which the beat appears, would converge each beat:

EXERCISE 14-9

With one or more of your classmates:

A   Tap or clap the basic beats in $\frac{3}{4}$ against $\frac{6}{8}$:

B   Tap or clap the "rhythm" in Example 14-23.
C   Sing or play Example 14-23.

Example 14-23.   **Legrant:** *Credo*

EXERCISE 14-10

A   Conduct or tap $\frac{3}{4}$, while one or more of your classmates conduct or tap $\frac{6}{8}$ and other classmates tap the common (♪).

B   Conduct or tap $\frac{4}{4}$, while one or more of your classmates conduct or tap $\frac{8}{8}$ ($\frac{3}{8} + \frac{3}{8} + \frac{2}{8}$) and other classmates tap the common (♪).

C   Conduct or tap $\frac{3}{4}$, while one or more of your classmates conduct or tap $\frac{5}{8}$ ($\frac{2}{8} + \frac{3}{8}$) and other classmates tap the common (♪).

D   Conduct or tap $\frac{4}{4}$, while one or more of your classmates conduct or tap $\frac{6}{4}$ and other classmates tap the following common pulse:

QUESTIONS AND
OBSERVATIONS

1   In which of the exercises do both meters converge in a simultaneous down-beat?
2   Can you feel two simultaneous meters at the same time?
3   Can any combination of meters be conceived of as a single simple or compound meter? Which ones?

4   Write these polymeters as a simple or compound meter, using accents to show the beat divisions.

5   Could any of these polymeters be conducted by one conductor? Which ones? Try it.

Simple polymeters that converge fairly regularly can be felt on the rhythmic level when they converge. Meters of $\frac{3}{4}$ and $\frac{6}{8}$ could be combined into a simple meter of $\frac{3}{4}$ ( ) or a compound meter of $\frac{6}{8}$ ( ).

EXERCISE 14-11

A   List other polymeters that could be combined into a single meter.

B   Conduct each rewritten form of these polymeters.

To Sum Up   Beats grouped in regular patterns in simple and some compound meters generate motion on the fastest moving time level. They are heard and felt as regular waves through tones and rests.

Irregular compound meters ($\frac{5}{8}$, $\frac{7}{8}$, $\frac{8}{8}$ [$\frac{3}{3} + \frac{3}{2} + \frac{2}{3}$ etc.]) that do not have even-grouped beats tend to be more unstable than meters with symmetrically grouped beats. But these compound meters become stabilized through the repetition of their asymmetrically grouped beats.

Polymeters that are closely related with beats or on a pulse that converge fairly regularly can be felt as a single simple or compound meter. Less related polymeters are felt as two distinct simultaneous meters.

PROJECT 14-1

Using Exercises 14-3 or 14-4 as musical material, write a "non-pitched" percussion piece that incorporates additional note values of different duration.

PROJECT 14-2

Using the rhythms of Exercise 14-4, write a melodic line for any soprano instrument. Write a simple accompaniment of one or two lines for other instruments, using slower-moving note values.

PROJECT 14-3

Using any exercise in Chapter 14 as musical material, write a short polymetric dance for percussion and/or percussion and piano.

PROJECT 14-4

Using any exercise in Chapter 14 as musical material, write a piece in compound meter. Use accents that *suggest* the polymeters contained within the compound meter. (Write for piano and/or solo instrument and percussion.)

LISTENING
SUGGESTIONS

Ives: *Three Places in New England,* second movement
Copland: *El Salón México*

Observe the polymetric sections. Is there a common beat? How often do the polymeters converge?

ANALYSIS 14-1

Find two musical examples of each of the following: simple meter, compound meter, and polymeter.

1 In each example, what is the relation of tempo to meter?
2 How do beats group themselves?
3 What are the strong, less strong, and weak beats?

15 METER:
Musical Aspects

OBJECTIVES

1. To *recognize* the relationship between beat and pulse.

2. To *study* the relationship between meter as a "small flow of time" and the musical "idea" (motive or line), harmony, and phrase.

CAPSULE DEFINITIONS

Syncopation	Displacement of the regular emphasis on the beat.
Metric modulation	A change from one meter and beat flow to another.

A. The Musical Function of Meter

In music, the meter, with its recurring beats and pulse, serves the musical function of generating motion at the fastest moving time level. Early church music, however, did not use meter, and some music of our day has abandoned meter as a musical element (here, for example, John Cage's *Fontana Mix*).

Let us examine the various rhythmic levels in Example 15-1.

Example 15-1.   **Mozart:** *Piano Sonata in C Major,* K. 545, first movement

The melodic/rhythmic flow in this example extends for two measures. The rhythm of the accompanying motive is half notes (𝅗𝅥 𝅗𝅥 | 𝅗𝅥 𝅗𝅥). The rhythm of the harmony is whole and half notes (𝅝 | 𝅗𝅥 𝅗𝅥) as it supports the rhythm of the melody.

The tempo (approximately) is ♩ = 120, or 𝅗𝅥 = 60. The 𝅗𝅥 pulse synchronizes with the accompaniment motive. It also coincides in part with the movement of the melody and harmony. The inner movement (or submovement) of the accompaniment is ♪ ♪ ♪ ♪ or ♪ 𝅗𝅥. = 𝅗𝅥 .

Each of these related time levels is emphasized by pitch levels. The pitch levels contain pulsations (or waves) that include both stressed and unstressed portions, which are comparable to strong vs. weak (as in scanning poetry), dōwn vs. ŭp, and attāck vs. dĕcay.

The stress and unstressed pulsations of the various time levels in the Mozart sonata might be diagramed as follows:

Melody:

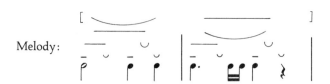

Accompaniment Motive: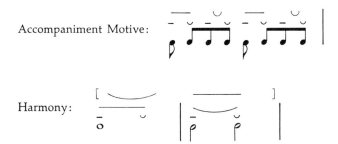

Harmony:

Observe that the subunits are all in the same basic duple meter.

EXERCISE 15-1

    A. Conduct Example 15-1 as follows:
       1. one gesture (beat) per measure
       2. two gestures (beats) per measure
       3. four gestures (beats) per measure
    B. Repeat A, accenting the strong beat of each measure while singing:
       1. the melody:

       2. the harmony:

RESULTS   The beat and the beat groupings in each bar (metrical level) are felt the most in the accompanying motive. Each stressed beat has an unstressed afterbeat. Even if the accompaniment motive were simplified

to 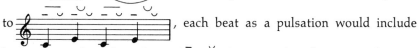 , each beat as a pulsation would include

both its attack and its decay (‿), stressed and unstressed. Even when the beat is absent briefly, like the pulse, we sense its continuing presence. However, if each beat is accented, our sense of the flow of other levels of musical time is impeded.

EXERCISE 15-2

    A Tap eight beats at a tempo of $\quad$ = 120. Stop, and then continue after a short break. Stop.
    B Play Example 15-2.

Example 15-2.   Beat groupings

C Repeat B, but shorten the rest to three beats.
D Repeat B, but lengthen the rest to five beats.
E Play Example 15-3.

Example 15-3.   Beat groupings

F Repeat E while the class taps continuous quarter notes.

QUESTIONS AND
OBSERVATIONS

1 What was your reaction to the silence in A? The whole-note rest in B? The three-beat rest in C? The five-beat rest in D? Does each alter the structure and meaning of the phrase? How?
2 What happened to the steady quarter-note beats in E? When did the change of meter in E become clearly heard and understood?
3 How do you interpret the meter(s) in F?

Once the steady quarter-note rhythm was set in motion, the expectation was that it would continue. The beat continued during the four-beat rest in B, as it did during the three-beat rest in C and the five-beat rest in D. But the first two measures established that there were four beats grouped together in each measure. Our expectation was that this pattern would continue. The three-beat rest disrupted this pattern and thwarted our expectation.

In E, the first measure established the quarter-note motion. Our expectation was that this pattern would continue. The eighth-note motion in measure 2 disrupted the quarter-note motion. Not until measures 3 and 4 could the change of meter and beat become established as a new pattern.

Once a pattern of beat and beat groupings and rests is established, there is an expectation that it will continue. A change in the pattern will be felt as a disturbance until it becomes established as the new pattern. This is true for tempo, rhythm, and meter, as it is for tonality and harmony.

Observe the changes in meter in Examples 15-4 and 15-5 and the changes of tempo in Example 15-5.

EXERCISE 15-3

Play or listen to, tap, or conduct:

A   Exercise 15-2D.
B   Example 15-4.
C   Example 15-5.

Example 15-4.   **Stravinsky:** *Symphonies of Wind Instruments*

Example 15-5.   **Webern:** *Variations for Orchestra*

QUESTIONS AND
OBSERVATIONS

1   Does the meter ever become stabilized in Examples 15-4 and 15-5?
2   Does the tempo ever become stabilized in Example 15-5?
3   Do you perceive larger rhythmic-flow patterns and metrical and tempo relationships as the music progresses?

Although the meter changes and the tempo alternates constantly in both examples, both eventually form larger, related rhythmic-flow patterns that become relatively stable (three-measure units in Example 15-4; measures 4–7 in Example 15-5).

B. Metrical Modulation

In tonal music, a change of key that is established becomes accepted as a *modulation*. Each modulation sets up its own patterns and expectations for its continuance and elaboration. Changes in tempo and meter serve to vary the time flow. To create a new key center or a change in the metrical time flow, a modulation must be made.

A metrical modulation is not simply a change of meter, as in Example 15-6, in which there is a common and recurring eighth-note beat. It is also an actual change of the speed of the beat.

EXERCISE 15-4

Examine Example 15-6.

Example 15-6.   **Ives:** *Sonata No. 1 for Violin and Piano* (two excerpts)

a.

b.

QUESTIONS AND
OBSERVATIONS

1   What is the basic beat in each measure?

2   Are these beats common to both measures in Example 15-6a? Both measures in Example 15-6b?

3   What is the common element in each example?

4   What is the counter-rhythm in measure 1 of Example 15-6b?

In Example 15-6a, a metrical modulation occurs in which the beat and meter change while the pulse (𝅗𝅥 = 𝅗𝅥.) remains the same. In Example 15-6b, a metrical modulation occurs in which the pulse and meter change while the beat of a counter-rhythm in $\frac{6}{4}$ (♩ ♩ ♩ ♩ ♩ ♩) becomes the basic beat in $\frac{4}{4}$ (♫ ♫ ♫ ♫). In both metrical modulations, the tempo is faster.

C. Syncopation

There is another way to disturb rather than alter an established time flow. We can change the position of the tones within the measure by placing them on the weak part of the beat, or on the *off*beat rather than *on* the beat. The beat pulsations are then contradicted; the roles of attack and decay are reversed. For the duration of this disturbance, there is an apparent change of beat. If this change is partial, affecting only one or two parts in the musical texture while other parts maintain clear beat patterns, the effect is called *syncopation*.

EXERCISE 15-5

A   Listen to the opening of Joplin's "Maple Leaf Rag."

B   Play and listen to Examples 15-7–15-9.

C   Mark the syncopations in Examples 15-7–15-9.

Example 15-7.   Schubert: *Symphony No. 8*, first movement

Example 15-8.   **Stravinsky:** *The Five Fingers,* No. 8

Example 15-9.   **Webern:** *Symphony*

1   In which part(s) does the syncopation occur in Examples 15-7–15-9?
    Is the effect similar in each case?

2   Are there clear beat patterns in the parts that are not syncopated?

3   Discuss the rhythmic treatment of the melody in Example 15-7.
    Which beat is emphasized in the melody? How is the first beat
    treated? What effect does this have on the syncopation?

Examples 15-7 and 15-8 and the "Maple Leaf Rag" contain a strong
first beat in the bass (emphasized by a tone or chord), which the syncopation can "play against." In Example 15-8, the syncopation on the second
beat (♫ ♩) of measure 1 helps to establish the dance character of the
tango, just as the syncopation in the "Maple Leaf Rag" establishes the
"ragged time" of ragtime. The beat flow is present in each case, and is
"played against" by the syncopation.

In the Schubert symphony, the bass has the first beat in each
measure. The syncopation in the accompaniment is not made explicit
until the melody enters (measure 3). And even here, the melody stresses
the second beat rather than the first.

In Example 15-9, Webern plays the syncopation off against a rest
on the first beat. How do we know it is a syncopation? The music can

be heard as $\frac{3}{4}$ () *until* measure 3 with

the low G. Then it doesn't seem to be in $\frac{3}{4}$ any more. The $\frac{2}{2}$ meter is

finally established with the G and what follows it:

The $\frac{2}{2}$ meter that is finally established in measure 3 permits us to hear $\frac{1}{2}$ = 50 as the pulse. The beats can now be heard clearly as "on" and "off."

The off beats give the music an extra "push" until the beat disturbance is resolved. But in the Webern symphony, the syncopation in its nonresolving function becomes as integral as the beat, which influences the ongoing shape of the piece.

EXERCISE 15-6

Take Exercise 14-3 or 14-4 and add to it a "rhythmic" supporting part that states the meter clearly, in regular beats. Alter the original line with syncopations.

In his *L'Histoire du Soldat*, Stravinsky uses both syncopation and changing meters to drive the music to a cadence and resolution.

EXERCISE 15-7

A   What is the basic beat in Example 15-10?
B   What is syncopated?
C   Where does the beat change?
D   Why is the time signature $\frac{3}{8}$ when the bass appears to be in $\frac{3}{4}$?

Example 15-10.   Syncopation and changing meters

RESULTS   The basic beat changes from ♩ to ♪ in the $\frac{3}{8}$, where a polymetric tension is created between bass and soprano. In one longer measure of $\frac{3}{4}$, the bass would be *on* the beat and the melody would be syncopated. In the two short measures of $\frac{3}{8}$, however, the melodic movement to e¹ ( ) is emphasized while on weak beats the bass acts as a syncopation until the resolution into $\frac{2}{4}$.

To Sum Up   Regularly grouped stressed and unstressed beats and pulses are heard and felt as regular pulsations through tones, intervals, chords, and rests.

A change of beat or pulse in which the beat appears on the unstressed part of the beat (the offbeat) rather than *on* the beat is felt as a syncopation if the regular pattern of beats or pulse is continued in another part.

An actual change of meter and beat/pulse that is eventually stabilized is felt as a metrical modulation with a new metric time flow.

Metrical modulations, syncopation, and irregular meters tend to drive the music onward and help to articulate and vary the shape-form as it evolves.

PROJECT 15-1

Write a short two-part instrumental piece in which each part has an independent rhythmic line in the same meter. Modulate metrically so that the counter-rhythm becomes the new basic rhythm.

PROJECT 15-2

Write a short ragtime piece (sixteen to thirty-two measures) that incorporates syncopation.

LISTENING
SUGGESTIONS

Stravinsky: *L'Histoire du Soldat,* first movement

Observe Stravinsky's use of meter.
What is the relationship between the meter, the movement of the music, and the structure of the phrases and cadences?

ANALYSIS 15-1

Review two works you have listened to previously. Observe the meter and its relationship to the movement of the music and the structure of phrases and cadences.

Find two examples of metrical modulation. Discuss the relationship between the meter and the beat before and after the metrical modulation.

BIBLIOGRAPHY: SECTION III

Cooper, Grosvenor W., and Leonard B. Meyer, *Rhythmic Structure of Music*. Chicago: University of Chicago Press, 1960.

Dunk, John L., *The Origin and Structure of Rhythm*. London: J. Clarke, 1952.

Hindemith, Paul, *A Composer's World*. Cambridge, Mass.: Harvard University Press, 1952.

Sachs, Curt, *Rhythm and Tempo*. New York: Norton, 1953.

Salzer, Felix, *Structural Hearing*. New York: Charles Boni, 1952.

Winckel, Fritz, *Music Sound and Sensation*. New York: Dover, 1967.

4 *Sound, Space, and Time*

GENERAL OBJECTIVE

1. To *develop* an awareness of the various levels of sound, space, and time in which music moves.

2. To *study* the relationship of melody, harmony, and rhythm in their various styles.

16

BASIC NOTIONS OF SOUND, SPACE, AND TIME

Our explorations of musical materials began with sound. Sound exists in real space and moves outward, creating musical space through tones, intervals, and chords; through "extra" tones—overtones and combination tones; and through nonpitched sounds. Each sound is related to and combines with other sounds in musical space from "high to low"; each creates new sounds while maintaining its own identity.

Sound exists in real time and extends outwards, creating musical time through melody, harmony, texture, rhythm, tempo, meter, and the resulting shape-form. From its inception, each sound contains certain tensions within itself and in relation to other sounds. These tensions set up expectations of future completion and resolution. These expectations are caused by the physical aspects of sound, those contained in the sound as overtones, combination tones, white noise, and so forth. They also come from historical associations—the way sounds have been used and organized through the various "systems," modal, tonal, and nontonal.

Sound and its elaboration on various musical levels results in shape-form. Our perception of this shape-form results both from the actual sounds that are produced and from our expectations of how they will be developed.

One level of musical sound is the *linear* or time-oriented level. In some cultures, this is the *only* level on which music exists. Another level of sound is the *vertical* or space-oriented level. Western music has continually evolved, widening its idea of sound, space, and time and its knowledge and acceptance of the various levels on which music can exist.

We have examined the vocabulary and some of the properties of sound in various spatial combinations—nonpitched, tonal, intervallic, and chordal—and how they extend in time—through rhythm, tempo, and meter. We must now explore the relationship of sounds to one another and their function and meaning on various musical levels as they evolve into a shape-form.

We therefore need to study the various musical levels on which sound can exist—the melodic, harmonic, and textural levels. We must also study *style*, the various ways (modal, tonal, and nontonal) in which sound can be organized.

Beethoven: Symphony No. 9, fourth movement

Note the melody in its unaccompanied form as a single line, and then in the various accompanied forms.

Léonin: "Organum" (plainsong)

Note the difference between the single line and the line "harmonized."

17 LINES IN TIME: Mode, Scale, and Key

OBJECTIVE

1. To *study* the interval structure of modes and scales in various keys as a basis for writing melodies and related harmonies.

CAPSULE DEFINITIONS

Mode; scale	Ordinarily, an arrangement of seven successive tones that span an octave with a fixed interval structure.
Church modes	Eight modes built on different tones.
Diatonic scales	Twelve major and minor scales built on different tones.
Key; tonality	A center or dominating tone upon which a scale is built, or to which various chords relate.
Key signature	Indicates the number of sharps or flats in a key.
Circle of fifths	A representation of key relationships that is determined by a progression of perfect fifths upward from C to C♯ and downward from C to C♭.
Modulation	Movement from one scale and key to another.
Tetrachord	Four successive ascending or descending tones.
Pentatonic scale	Five-tone scale.
Whole-tone scale	Six-tone scale.

A. Preliminary Explorations

The music of various times and cultures has been based on and related to the scale forms then current. Gregorian chant and organum were based on the church modes. The baroque concerto and the classical symphony were based on the diatonic major and minor scale forms (an outgrowth of the Aeolian and Ionian modes). Scale forms of various cultures East and West, including the chromatic scale, continue to be used in twentieth-century music.

All scale forms have some characteristics in common. One is a predominating tone that acts as the *key tone.* This tone, from which other scale tones ascend and descend by various intervals, defines the key, or *tonal center.* Because there are twelve different halfsteps in the chromatic scale, there are twelve possible key tones or tonal centers upon which to construct scales. Most scales are built on successive seconds. The specific size of each successive second is crucial to the structure of the scale.

B. Modes

The *ecclesiastical* or *church modes,* which were modifications of the early Greek modes, were the basic scale forms used in medieval music. These modes include four *authentic modes* and four related *plagal modes,* which begin a fourth below their authentic counterparts. Each of the four authentic modes begins on a new tone (see Example 17-1).

Example 17-1.   Authentic modes

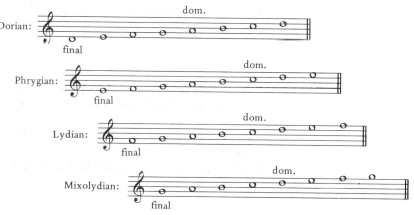

EXERCISE 17-1

> A Sing or play each of the authentic modes.
> B Analyze the interval structure of each.

In the sixteenth century, Glareanus, a sixteenth century theorist and philosopher, recognized three additional modes that were also in use (see Example 17-2).

Example 17-2.   Additional modes

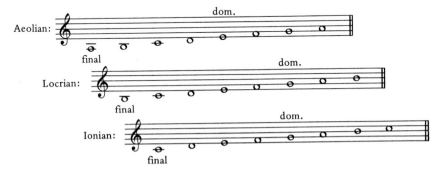

EXERCISE 17-2

> A Sing each of the three modes in Example 17-2.
> B Analyze the interval structure of each.
> C What are the common characteristics of the seven modes? What are the differences?

RESULTS   The seven modes in Examples 17-1 and 17-2 are referred to as the *diatonic modes*. Each is built on a different tone and has a different interval structure with a different arrangement of its major and minor seconds. The range of each mode is one octave.

EXERCISE 17-3

> A Construct the seven diatonic modes on the *same* tone, transposing each mode and altering tones when necessary to preserve the interval structure of each.
> B Compare the transposed modes. What are their similarities? Their differences?
> C Which modes are most similar to the Aeolian mode? The Ionian mode?

EXERCISE 17-4

Using the Aeolian and Ionian modes as models, alter the interval structure of each mode in Exercise 17-3 so that it becomes either the Aeolian or Ionian mode.

RESULTS   The crucial interval that distinguishes the Ionian and Aeolian modes is the third above the key tone. Although each mode has a different interval structure, the modes divide into two basic types—those resembling the Ionian (with the *major* third above the key tone) and those resembling the Aeolian (with the *minor* third above the key tone). These two types of modes are basically the same as our major and minor scales, respectively.

Three other tones in each mode play important functions. The fifth tone in the Dorian, Lydian, Mixolydian, Aeolian, and Ionian modes is the *dominating* tone. The *sixth* tone in the Phrygian and Locrian modes is the *dominating* tone. The seventh tone and the dominating tone ordinarily resolve to the *final,* or key tone (referred to in later music as the *tonic*). The *final* is ordinarily the starting and ending tone of a piece.

EXERCISE 17-5

A   Examine Examples 17-3–17-7.

Example 17-3.   "All the Pretty Little Horses" (folk song)

etc.

Example 17-4.   " Kyrie IV: Cunctipotens" (Gregorian chant) (H.A.M. 15)

Ky-ri   e   e -   le - i - son

Example 17-5.   Balbulus: "Alleluia" (H.A.M. 16)

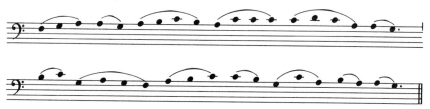

Example 17-6.   *"L'Homme armé"* (folk song) (H.A.M. 66a)

Example 17-7.   **Dufay:** *Missa, "L'Homme armé": Kyrie I* (two excerpts) (H.A.M. 66b)

a.

b.

B   What is the mode of each example?

C   What is the final, and what is the dominating tone?

D   How do the final and the dominating tone function in these examples?

E   What is the relationship between Examples 17-6 and 17-7?

RESULTS   Example 17-3 is in the Aeolian mode transposed, Examples 17-4 and
17-6 are in the Dorian mode, and Example 17-5 is in the Lydian mode.

In Examples 17-4 and 17-5, much of the melody revolves around
the dominating tone. In the former example the melody resolves to the
final; in the latter it does not.

Dufay, a fifteenth-century composer, used the "L'Homme armé"
melody (Example 17-6) as a *cantus firmus.* Although the cantus firmus
is based on the transposed Dorian mode, it contains alterations that
change the interval structure of the mode (F♯ in measure 7, B♮ in
measures 16 and 17).

As the medieval and Renaissance composer oriented himself more towards harmony, the modes were often modified by accidentals (♯, ♭)—which were called *musica ficta*—and were transposed to other pitch areas (see Example 17-7).

As the characteristics of the major and minor third of the modes became more predominant, the subtle distinctions between the modes became less important. The two basic scale forms that finally emerged were the major and minor scales.

C. Scales

The starting tone of a scale is the *central* dominating tone, to which all others relate. Because there are twelve different tones, any tone can serve as the key tone. What is lost in the intervallic subtlety of the modes is gained in the *key flexibility* of the scale forms. But the minor scale does retain some of the intervallic flexibility and subtlety of the modes while being dominated by its key tone.

Minor Scales

EXERCISE 17-6

A Sing or play the following ascending and descending forms of the minor scale:

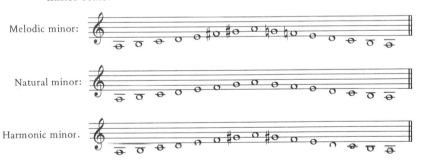

Melodic minor:

Natural minor:

Harmonic minor:

B Analyze the interval structure of each.
C What authentic modes are related to each of these minor scales?
D What do these three scales have in common that identifies them as minor scales?
E What is the essential difference between minor and major scales?

EXERCISE 17-7

A Play Examples 17-8–17-10.

B   On which form of the minor scale is each example based?

C   What is the key signature or number of sharps or flats of each? How do you determine the number of sharps or flats of each?

Example 17-8.   **Haydn:** *Symphony No. 2 (104),* andante

Example 17-9.   **Mozart:** *Symphony No. 40,* allegro

Example 17-10.   **Bach:** *"Erschienen ist der herrliche Tag,"* chorale prelude

   etc.

RESULTS

Example 17-8 is based on the *harmonic* minor scale whose interval structure is based on the lowered sixth and raised seventh. Example 17-9 is based on the *descending melodic* minor scale, which has the same interval structure as the natural minor scale ascending *and* descending (lowered sixth, lowered seventh). Example 17-10 is based on the *melodic* minor scale ascending (raised sixth and seventh) and descending (lowered sixth and seventh). Each minor scale contains a minor third. The Dorian and Phrygian modes share the minor third with all the minor scales. The natural minor is equivalent to the Aeolian mode. The lower third, sixth, and seventh of the natural minor scale (minor third, sixth, and seventh) give the accidentals that will be included in the key signature of all minor scales.

Other Scale Forms

The major and minor scales are seven-tone scales. Some other scales use fewer tones.

EXERCISE 17-8

A   Sing or play Examples 17-11–17-14.

B   Describe their interval structure.

C   For each example, construct a scale that incorporates the tones in the example. How many tones in each scale?

D   Do any of the scales in C have a relationship to any modes or scales? If so, which ones?

E Is there a key tone in each scale? If so, what is it?

F Keep each tone, but transpose each scale in C up to its next scale step.

G Does the key tone of each scale remain the same? Is there a relationship between the scale and *other* modes or scales? If so, which ones?

H Construct three other scales, of seven tones each based on different interval structures. You may use existing or synthetic scales.

I Sing or play each of the scale forms in C and H.

Example 17-11.   "The Good Old Way," from *The Southern Harmony*

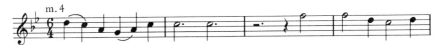

Example 17-12.   **Yannatos:** *"Snow Is Flowing Down," Collection of Songs Based on Children's Poems*

Example 17-13.   **Debussy:** *Nocturnes:* "Fêtes"

Example 17-14.   **Wagner:** *Tristan and Isolde,* prelude

RESULTS   Examples 17-11 and 17-12 are based on the *pentatonic* (five-tone) *scale*. The former is in F major, the latter in C major. Example 17-13 is based on a *whole-tone scale*. Since there are no half steps in the whole-tone scale or in this specific pentatonic scale (there are forms that include half steps) to act as a leading tone, *any* tone could be the key tone. In the *chromatic scale* upon which Example 17-13 is based, there are *only* half steps; *any* tone could act as a leading tone. We must examine the tones in relation to the keys (A major, C major) and their harmonies in order to determine how they function in the piece.

To Sum Up   Modal music is based on the intervallic structure of the modes. Tonal music is based on the intervallic structure of the scales. The more flexible forms of the minor scales retain some of the modal flavor, while being controlled by a key tone. Scales that can be built on any of the twelve tones are tonally more flexible than the modes which are confined to seven diatonic tones.

Scales other than major and minor can be built on any pitch. Examples are the pentatonic (five-tone) scale, the whole-tone (six-tone) scale, and the chromatic (twelve-tone) scale. Music based on a key tone is not necessarily confined to that center, since it could *modulate* to pitch levels where other key tones dominate.

D. Scale and Key Extension: Modulation

A piece of music can be built on one or more scale forms. Since a scale can be built on any pitch, there must be a way to get from one scale form to another smoothly and without stopping. There must be a way to shift to another pitch level or key and start the new scale. The process of moving from one scale form to another has traditionally been called *modulation*. Exercises 17-9 and 17-10 explore the various ways scales can be extended through simple forms of modulation.

EXERCISE 17-9

Examine the C major scale:

A   What is the interval structure of this scale?

B   What is the relationship between tones 1–4 and 5–8?

C   Construct a scale in which g (tone *5* of the C major scale) is the center tone (tone *1*). Maintain the same interval structure as in the C major scale.

D   Using tone *5* in G as a new starting tone (tone *1*), construct another scale.

E   Continue this process until you return to your starting tone c. For example, use tone *5* of a D major scale, as tone 1 for an A major scale. (Transpose down one or two octaves when necessary rather than extending the staff.)

F   List the name of each scale and the number and name of the accidentals contained in each.

EXERCISE 17-10

A   Construct a scale in which you use c′ to f′ as the *second* half of an

F major scale (), descending by step to f.

B   Continue this process, descending by step until you return to your starting tone c. (Transpose *up* one or two octaves when necessary rather than extending the staff.)

C   List the name of each scale and the accidentals contained in each.

QUESTIONS AND
OBSERVATIONS

1   Do you note any relationship between certain sharp and flat keys? Describe.

2   What is the relationship between a scale and its key signature?

Scales can be extended in either direction. Each diatonic scale contains two intervallically similar *tetrachords*, which have four tones each. Ascending by fifths, the second tetrachord, which begins on tone *5* (always the *dominant* in tonal music) can act as the first tetrachord, tone *5* becoming a new tone *1* of a new scale. Descending by fifths, the first tetrachord, which begins on tone *1* and ends on tone *4*, can act as the second tetrachord: tone *4* (transposed down one octave and called the *subdominant*) becomes the new tone *1*. In each case, we have *modulated* from one scale to another. Modulation will be discussed in detail in Chapter 20.

EXERCISE 17-11

Use Exercises 17-9 and 17-10 to construct a *circle of fifths* that graphically represents key relationships.

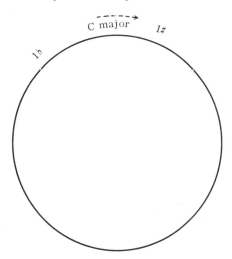

E. The Relationship Between Major and Minor Scales

Each minor scale is related to a particular major scale. Scales with the same key signature are called *relative scales;* the minor relative is written a minor third below the major scale. Scales that begin on the same tone but have different key signatures are called *parallel scales.*

EXERCISE 17-12

A Use the natural minor-scale form in Exercise 17-6 to construct the relative minor scales of major scales in Exercise 17-9, C–E, ascending by fifths.

B List the names of each minor scale and the accidentals contained in each.

C Alter A so as to form the harmonic minor-scale forms.

QUESTIONS AND OBSERVATIONS

1 What is the relation between parallel *C major* and *C minor* scales?

2 Parallel *A major* and *A minor* scales?

3 Parallel *E major* and *E minor* scales?

4 Would you be able to tell the signatures of the melodic and harmonic forms of the minor scale? What problems would you confront?

Minor scales are more flexible in their intervallic make-up. But they are also less stable than their major counterparts, which sets up interesting harmonic problems in the construction of chords in minor keys.

The various major and minor scale forms serve both melodic and harmonic functions. With their common tetrachords (based on common tones), they can easily modulate from one scale and key to another.

The chromatic scale, by continual alterations (♯, ♭) of the diatonic scales, is tonally flexible and can modulate easily from one key to another.

EXERCISE 17-11
(VARIATION)

Place the names of the appropriate minor scales under their related major-scales.

PROJECT 17-1

Write three four-to-eight-measure vocal melodies with different melodic contours. Base each melody on a church mode, and use essentially stepwise motion. Stress those tones that give the melody a particular modal flavor by positioning them in appropriate places in the melody and by lengthening their duration. Harmonize each melody with one or two other voices, using *only* the tones of the mode on which the melody is based. Watch voice leading, resolving intervals or chords as they require it.

PROJECT 17-2

Write three four-to-eight-measure flexible instrumental melodies. Base each melody on a major or minor form of a scale, using skips as well as stepwise motion. Harmonize each melody for piano or two or three other instruments, using chords derived from the tones of the scale. (The chordal accompaniment should be simple.)

ANALYSIS 17-1

A   Look at four pieces—a Baroque, a Classical, a Romantic, and either a folk or popular piece. Play or listen to each. On what scale is each based? Do they begin and end in the same key? Are *other* keys included in the same piece? If so, which keys?

B   Find other examples of the pentatonic scale in the folk or popular repertory.

LISTENING
SUGGESTIONS

"Christmas Cycle" (plainchant)
Dufay: *Alma redemptoris Mater*
Palestrina: *Pope Marcellus Mass*

On what mode(s) or key does each seem to be based?

18 *LINES IN TIME:*
Motives, Melodies, and Tonality

OBJECTIVES

1. To *study* the relationship between tones in a melody.
2. To *write* simple melodies.

CAPSULE DEFINITIONS

Goal tone	A tone (usually at the cadence) to which other tones gravitate.
Sprechstimme	"Speech-song."
Motive	A short, cohesive melodic/rhythmic unit of two or more tones.
Phrase unit	A cohesive grouping of tones within a phrase. (Two phrase units could constitute a phrase.)
Theme	A line or melody that functions in relation to other lines or melodies.
Augmentation	A group of tones in a motive or melody whose durations are lengthened.
Diminution	A group of tones in a motive or melody whose durations are shortened.

A. Preliminary Explorations

A tone, succession of tones, mode, or scale establishes certain expectations of elaboration and completion. Starting a piece on d' in the fourteenth century and in the eighteenth century led to very different results. Musical language evolves and changes. The way a composer works with and organizes his musical material influences the evolution of the language.

In the context of eighteenth-century scales and keys, a piece beginning on d' could be expected to move up to e' or down to c♯'. If d' moved to e', the next likely tone would be f' or f♯'; f♯' would most likely move to g', but f♮' might move to g' or e'. Continuing upward from g', what tones might follow?

The elements of rhythm and harmony can help resolve ambiguities by stressing certain tones and their movement up or down. There are still *ton*-al choices, given the limited context of a scale (stepwise, ascending, descending) and depending upon the interval structure of the major-scale forms and the natural, harmonic, or melodic minor-scale forms.

Of course, melodies based on modes or scales are not confined to limited stepwise up-and-down motion. Examples 18-1–18-4 are all based on a particular mode or scale, each with a different arrangement of steps and skips.

EXERCISE 18-1

Play or sing Examples 18-1–18-4.

Example 18-1.   **Beethoven:** *Violin Concerto*, first movement

Example 18-2.   **J. S. Bach:** *Partita in D Minor for Solo Violin*

193

Example 18-3.   *"Benedicamus Domino"* (plainsong) (H.A.M. 28)

Be - ne - di - ca - mus   Do

Example 18-4.   **Mozart:** *Don Giovanni:* "Batti, Batti"

QUESTIONS AND
OBSERVATIONS

1   On what mode or scale forms are these melodies based?

2   In what ways do they conform to the limited expectations required of the mode or scale upon which they are based? In what ways do they differ?

3   Do some tones appear more important than others? Why?

4   In each example, mark the melodic contour and each phrase or phrase unit. How do these elements relate to each other?

Each melody in Examples 18-1–18-4 is based on the tones of a particular mode or scale. The motion of the tones in each melody includes skips as well as stepwise motion. Observe the interval of each skip, its relative stability, the two tones involved, and their movement and resolution after the skip. Observe where the skip occurs within the structure of the melody. Observe the relationship of the tones to the key.

The interval of successive seconds is very important in the construction of any modal or tonal melody. But other intervals must also be used for interest and variety.

Exercise 18-1 has shown that there are tones within each melody (and related scale) that are more important than others and towards which other tones gravitate. These tones are called *goal tones.* Goal tones occur in crucial places within or at the end of the phrase. They contribute to the chord and emphasize the structural relationship of the tone and chord to the *key.* (See Examples 18-5–18-8.)

Example 18-5.   Goal tones in Example 18-1, mm. 2 and 4

I (tonic)

V (dominant)

Example 18-6.   Goal tone in Example 18-2

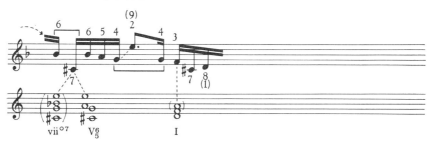

Example 18-7.   Goal tones in Example 18-3

Example 18-8.   Goal tones in Example 18-4, mm. 2 and 4

Each of the tonal melodies (Examples 18-1, 18-2, and 18-4) moved by step to the first goal tone (at the end of a phrase unit), skipping to extend the cadence (Example 18-1: 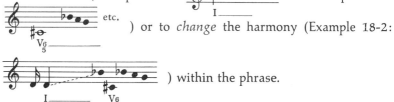 and Example 18-2:

etc.) or to *change* the harmony (Example 18-2:

) within the phrase.

In Example 18-4, the first goal tone, f′, resolved by step to e′ on the weak part of the second beat, after the change of harmony. The skip to b♭ began the second phrase unit on the same chord (V).

In Example 18-3, the first goal tone, d, was reached by skip and stepwise motion ( ) extended at the cadence melodically.

Each goal tone in Examples 18-1–18-4 was a breathing point within or at the end of the melodic/rhythmic contour that resulted in a cohesive phrase or phrase unit.

B. Motives

Included in many melodies are smaller melodic/rhythmic units called *motives*. In Example 18-9, these smaller melodic/rhythmic units start *after* each melodic dip of e♭¹, g′, and c².

Example 18-9.   **Beethoven:** *Symphony No. 5*, first movement, m. 6

Any short cohesive melodic/rhythmic unit of two or more tones is called a motive. Each motive has an identifiable shape, which is defined by a specific interval, direction, and rhythmic pattern.

A motive can introduce a melody or theme (Examples 18-10 and 18-11).

Example 18-10.   **Haydn:** *Symphony No. 2*, adagio

Example 18-11.   **Beethoven:** *Symphony No. 5*, first movement

A motive can also act as a "germ," generating a melody or larger musical section by:

1 *repetition*—exact or sequential (Example 18-9).
2 *variation*—inversion (Example 18-12A and 18-13A); augmentation (Example 18-12B).
3 *alternation* with another motive(s) (Examples 18-13b and 18-14).

Example 18-12.   **Brahms:** *Symphony No. 4*, first movement, (two excerpts)

a.

b.

Example 18-13.   **Webern:** *Variations for Orchestra*, measure 21–26, (two excerpts)

a.

b.

Example 18-14.   **Mozart:** *Symphony No. 40*, first movement

EXERCISE 18-2

A   Play Examples 18-12–18-14.
B   What is the key of Examples 18-12a, 18-12b, and 18-14?
C   Which tones are structurally most important in this key?
D   Mark the interval structure of the motives contained in the melody of each example.
E   How is stepwise, skipwise motion used by the composer?
F   Mark the temporary goal tones.
G   Which goal tone pushes the melody onward? Which resolves the melody, if only momentarily?
H   What is the range of each piece?

RESULTS

In Example 18-14, Mozart uses repetitions of motive A to generate the melodic line. An insistent rhythm of ♪♪♩ and a dissonant interval of a minor second creates an ongoing tension, which is intensified by the skip to the temporary goal tone or tonic bb^2. Motive B extended by motive C (a variant of motive A) resolves finally to the goal tone c^2.

In Example 18-12, the major-third and minor-third skips create the need for larger major-sixth and minor-sixth counter-skips to move the melody forward.

Example 18-13 is *not* in a tonal style. Therefore, the hierarchies of a melodic and harmonic tonal order—with certain tones being more significant structurally than others—do not necessarily apply. Therefore one's expectations can be "out of phase" with the actual music. The entire melody is based on skips to the goal tones c^2 and $c\sharp^3$ (Example 18-13a) and c', $g\flat'$, and $a\flat$ (Example 18-13b).

In Examples 18-12–18-14, each composer works with the *properties* of the intervals (tonal and nontonal style) and the rhythm to propel the motive forward. Each uses skips, counterbalancing skips, goal tones, either stepwise motion (Example 18-14) or *transposed* stepwise motion (Example 18-13), and a range that fits the motive. Each creates tension, a degree of resolution, and the need for the motive's elaboration and development until its completion and final cadence.

A motive can serve harmonic as well as melodic functions. Many accompanying figures are based on a repeated motive. (See Examples 8-17, 8-18, and 8-21, 8-22.)

In both melodic and accompanying roles, the motive is subject to harmonic as well as melodic forces. This is true in tonal as well as nontonal music.

PROJECT 18-1

Compose a short piece based on a motive that is extended by repetition—exact, sequential, inverted, augmented, or compressed—for solo violin (optional accompaniment by percussion or piano). Keep in mind the motive's rhythmic movement in relation to its melodic and harmonic elements.

PROJECT 18-2

Starting with a very short sentence (such as "I walk."), add other bits of information ("to the store," "with my dog," "slowly," "because," etc.). Set the sentence rhythmically for voice, using approximate pitch in the form of the inflective *Sprechstimme*. (Accompaniment is optional.)

LISTENING
SUGGESTIONS

Beethoven: Symphony No. 5, first movement
Brahms: Symphony No. 4, first movement
Schoenberg: Pierrot Luniare

C. Simple Melodies

Melodies can be based on scales yet not be limited by their rigid structure. They can be based on broken chords. They can be based on motives that are extended through repetition, variation, and alternation. Melodies can be extremely short or seemingly endless. They can be written in a modal, tonal, or nontonal style.

Each melody is a succession of related tones that are ordered rhythmically. Each develops into a coherent and recognizable shape in time and space.

Each melody, short or long, needs time to "breathe." It needs cadences to which to move and in which to resolve and gather up energy to move on. This is true for both vocal and instrumental music.

Each melody is conceived vocally and/or instrumentally. Physical limitations and possibilities must be considered in constructing the melody. The range, quality, and number of voices and/or instruments and the *type* of piece (chamber, symphonic, operatic, etc.) affect the kind of melody that is composed.

A simple melody is short: it consists of at least two to four phrases that resolve in a full cadence. A melody can function within a piece in a variety of ways:

1.   It can extend the length of the piece (Example 18-15).
2.   It can be the first part of a two-part piece (Example 18-16), or it can extend throughout the piece.
3.   It can be the first part of a three-part piece and return in the third part (Example 18-17), or it can extend throughout the piece.
4.   It can be a first or second theme in a larger work (Example 18-18).
5.   It can be a theme of a larger piece, serving as the first part of a two- or three-part section of the piece and return in the second or third part, or it can extend throughout the two or three part section of the piece (Example 18-19).

Example 18-15.   **Billings:** *"Chester"*

Example 18-16.   **J. S. Bach:** *Little Notebook for Anna Magdalena Bach,* aria

Example 18-17.   **Foster:** *"Oh! Susanna"*

Example 18-18.   **Beethoven:** *Violin Concerto,* first movement, theme 2

Example 18-19.   **Mozart:** *Piano Sonata,* K. 331

EXERCISE 18-3

A   Play and examine Examples 18-15–18-19.
B   What is the key of each piece?
C   Which tones are most important structurally in this key? In this piece?
D   What is the relationship of a tone's length to its structural function?
E   In each melody, mark the melodic contours and rhythmic patterns that are similar.
F   Mark phrases and cadence points when necessary. Observe those phrases that are basically similar. What is their relationship to one another?
G   How is stepwise and skipwise motion used?
H   Are there scale patterns and chord patterns in the melodies?

RESULTS   Each melody is made of small units of either stepwise scale patterns or broken chords that form into melodic contours and create melodic movement. Within each melody, there is a great deal of repetition of melodic/rhythmic patterns. Rhythmically, each melody moves from quicker moving to slower moving stressed tones within the measure and within the phrase. These stressed tones are important to the tonal structure of the phrase because they outline melodic as well as harmonic movement throughout the phrase.

Each melody can be extended by the addition of complementary phrases in which the original phrase is *repeated* but *varied* at the cadence (Examples 18-17 and 18-18); *inverted* (phrase unit in Example 18-18); or *contrasted* (Examples 18-15 and 18-16).

Each of the simple melodies in Examples 18-15–18-19 moves within a tonality and is confined to the melodic and harmonic relationships of that tonality.

In exploring melody further, we must consider harmony and its relationship to melody.

PROJECT 18-3

Construct a simple melody of at least two phrases for voice and accompanying instrument (guitar, piano, etc). Base your composition on the melodic minor scale. Place structurally important tones (tonic, dominant, subdominant, and leading tone) in prominent places within and at the end of phrases. Use any of Examples 18-15–18-19 as a model.

PROJECT 18-4

Construct a melody for piano based on broken chords. Use stepwise motion to balance the various skips. Use any of the previous examples in this chapter as a model. Or use Beethoven: Piano Sonata, Op. 2, No. 2, first movement; or Bartók, Mikrokosmos, Volume 3, No. 79 or No. 85. To support your melody, write an accompaniment based on a motive.

LISTENING
SUGGESTION

Beethoven: Violin Concerto, first movement

Observe the themes that Beethoven uses—their character, their tonality, their range, their treatment when played by the solo violin, and their treatment when played by the orchestra.

In addition, take three pieces you have already heard. This time, listen while examining the score. Observe the tonality, melody, phrase lengths, motives, harmony, and instrumentation of each piece.

19 *LINES AND CHORDS IN TIME*

OBJECTIVES

1. To *study* the relationship between tones, intervals, and chords that serve melodic, harmonic, and tonal functions.

2. To *study* the different forms of cadences as they are used to articulate phrase structure and the form of a piece.

3. To *write* melodies, supported by harmonies that move to goal tones and cadences.

CAPSULE DEFINITIONS

Primary chords	I	IV	V
Secondary chords	ii	iii	vi ˙ vi

Cadences				
complete	{	*authentic* =	V	I
		plagal =	IV	I
incomplete	{	*half* =	IV	V
		=	I	V
		=	ii	V
		deceptive =	V	vi

Nonchord tones	Melodic tones that do not belong to the supporting harmony.
Harmonic rhythm	The movement of the harmony.

A. Preliminary Explorations

In Chapters 8–10, we explored the chord vocabulary and the melodic aspects of chord progressions. Melodic aspects included the melodic movement of tones within the chord—voice leading, common tones, doubling of chord tones, and movement from chord to chord. Any single chord, like any single tone, is ambiguous until it is related to other chords and tones in a musical context. Tones, intervals, and chords are the composer's vocabularly, though they have no specific literal meaning, as words do.

Each chord in a progression, then, like each tone in a melody, derives its meaning from its function in a musical context. Each must be examined in relation to its surrounding tones or chords.

EXERCISE 19-1

Play or sing each of the following:

1   Did you expect other tones or chords to follow those in each example?

2   What does the g (   ) "mean"? How does it function melodically in B–E?

3   What does the G major triad (   ) "mean"? How does it function harmonically in F–J?

G' or a G major triad, for example, could be found in many melodic and harmonic progressions in various musical styles. Each musical situation varies, as does each musical style. There is always a musical grammar, a syntax relating musical elements, within a particular style. The *meaning* of g' or a G major triad in a melodic or harmonic progression is a result of (1) its relationship with other tones or chords in the progression and (2) its function within the particular musical style of that progression.

B. Stressed Tones: Primary Triads; The Phrase

In Examples 18-1–18-4, certain tones were more important than other tones. The position of these tones in the melody, their duration, their position in the scale, and their relation to the key all stressed the importance of their function and meaning in the structure of the melody and in outlining the melodic movement within the phrase.

In the scales and chords we have examined, we found certain basic relationships that existed throughout the tonal system. Each fifth tone of the scale or dominant chord (V) of a key could be a new prime tone (1) or *tonic* chord (I) for the next ascending key. Each fourth tone or subdominant chord (IV) could be a new prime tone (1) or tonic chord (I) for the next descending key.

I, IV, and V (or IV → I ← V) are called *primary chords.* Like the melodic stressed tones, these chords are structurally the most important chords within a key. Each primary chord, with its inversions, helps establish a key and stabilize a phrase. Each primary chord a fifth above or below the tonic could become a new key center.

Examples 19-1–19-4 contain various chords in different positions.

EXERCISE 19-2

    A   Play or listen to Examples 19-1–19-4.

    B   Mark the chord names and/or numerals under each chord in the four examples.

    C   Which are primary chords? Describe how they stabilize the phrase.

    D   Mark the phrase/cadence in each example.

Example 19-1.   **Billings:** *"Chester"*

Example 19-2.   **Bach:** *"Aus Meines Herzens Grunde"* (chorale)

Example 19-3.   **Rimsky-Korsakov:** *Sheherazade, II*

a.

Rimsky-Korsakov: *Sheherazade, IV*

b.

Example 19-4.   **Beethoven:** *Piano Sonata*, Op. 2, No. 2, second movement

etc.

1   What chords end each phrase?
2   Which cadences sound complete? Which sound incomplete?
3   What position (1, 3, or 5) do the melody tones occupy in the cadence chords?
4   Are there some tones that do not fit into a chord?
5   What is the rhythm of the harmony?
6   What is the relationship of the tempo to the harmonic rhythm?

Examples 19-2 and 19-4 end the period (phrase I and phrase II) with a complete cadence: V–I (authentic cadence).

Example 19-3b ends the phrase with a complete cadence: IV–I (plagal cadence).

Examples 19-1, 19-2, and 19-4 end the first phrase with an incomplete cadence: I–V (half cadence).

Example 19-3a ends the phrase with an incomplete cadence: V–VI (deceptive cadence).

Incomplete cadences (*half* and *deceptive*) that end the first phrase are usually resolved with *complete cadences* (*authentic* and *plagal*) at the end of the second phrase or period.

EXERCISE 19-3

A   Find at least one example of each cadence in other pieces.
B   Using at least four chords in three or four parts, write an example of each cadence in F-sharp minor, A-flat major, G minor, and B major.

C. Harmonic Extensions: Secondary Triads; Phrase Extension

Although primary chords state the harmonic structure within a tonality, they need other chords called secondary chords to help prolong and develop the phrase. In Exercises 19-4–19-7 primary and secondary chords in both major and minor are used to explore various possible harmonic progressions.

EXERCISE 19-4

A   Insert secondary chords (and their first inversions) between the following primary chords so as to prolong the phrase. (Use Examples 19-1–19-4 as models).

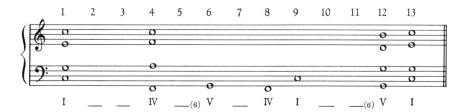

B   Play or sing the result with your classmates.

QUESTIONS AND
OBSERVATIONS

1   Describe root movement, voice leading, common tones, and chord progression in Exercise 19-4.

2   In which position (1, 3, or 5) within each secondary chord do you find important structural tones? Within each primary chord? Which group of chords (primary or secondary) has more structurally important tones?

EXERCISE 19-5

A   Rewrite Exercise 19-4 in C minor, using chords based on the harmonic minor form.

B   Which triads are now major? Which are minor?

C   Do the same basic progressions work as well in minor as they do in major?

D   Do secondary chords seem as stable as primary chords in a major key? Why? In a minor key? Why?

Secondary triads can also *substitute* for primary triads, in order to:

1   vary and prolong the phrase structure.

2   forestall an expected cadence (deceptive cadence).

Any secondary triad that has two tones in common with the primary triad can assume this *substitute* function.

We know that chords can progress by *step* or by *skip* (I–ii, etc., or I–VI–IV, etc.), or by a combination of *step* and *skip* (I–ii–V–iii–VI, etc., or I–V–ii–VI–iii, etc.).

EXERCISE 19-6

A   Write a harmonic progression based on combinations of steps and skips that ends in a plagal cadence.

B   Play or sing A with your classmates.

C Which progressions move well? Which seem unsatisfactory? Why?

D Revise A, correcting unsatisfactory chord choices, voice leading, doublings, and so on.

EXERCISE 19-7

A Write another version of Exercise 19-4, 19-5, or 19-6, substituting secondary triads for some primary triads in root position or first inversion.

B Play or sing both versions with your classmates.

C Describe the differences in sound and function between the chords of the two versions.

RESULTS Each of the primary chords is crucial in clarifying the shape-form of the piece. The primary chords establish the key. They occur at cadences, and this gives the piece a clear, ongoing direction.

Secondary triads function like unstressed tones: they prolong the phrase, vary the tonal and chordal vocabulary, and delay expected cadences.

PROJECT 19-1

Set Example 19-5 in four parts for voices, using primary and secondary triads with appropriate cadences. Name and/or mark chord functions.

Example 19-5. *"Come, Come Ye Saints"* (Mormon hymn)

Fine

D.C. al Fine

PROJECT 19-2

    A Starting with the bass in Example 19-6, write two or three additional parts for the piano, using appropriate chords and inversions. Name and/or mark each chord function.

    B Arrange A for three or four different instruments, transposing it if necessary.

Example 19-6.   Chord construction

D. Melodic Chord Tones—Melodic Nonchord Tones—Melodic Extension

In Examples 19-2 and 19-4, you must have been aware that there were some tones that did not "fit" into the basic chord structure. These *nonchord tones* appeared to move at a quicker pace than the harmony. Exercises 19-8–19-10 examine chord tones and nonchord tones as they affect the relationship of the melody to the harmony and the melodic rhythm to the harmonic rhythm.

Example 19-7.   **Mozart:** *Piano Sonata*, K. 331

EXERCISE 19-8

A In Example 19-7, do the tones of the melody in any particular measure suggest a complete chord? If not, what tones are needed to complete the chord? Circle the tones in the melody that belong to the chord.

B Which chords are primary chords? Which are secondary chords?

C Which chords are in root position? Which are inverted?

D Which chords and/or their inversions are stable? Which are less stable? How are each of these chords used?

E Where is the greatest degree of tension in the phrase? Why? How does the tension build to this point?

F Describe the melodic aspects of the harmony.

Example 19-8.   **Beethoven:** *Violin Concerto,* first movement, theme 2

EXERCISE 19-9

A In Example 19-8, do the tones in the melody in any measure or group of measures suggest a complete chord? Which chord(s)?

B If so, are the chords suggested by the tones in the melody the same as the basic chord structure of the harmony?

C Circle those chord tones in the melody that belong to the basic chord structure of the harmony.

D On what beat (or part of the beat) in the measure is each of these chord tones placed?

E What are the tones before and after each chord tone?

F How do they function in the melody?

  G Are they consonant with the harmony?

  H Does the harmonic rhythm move more quickly (that is, with quicker note values) than the melodic rhythm?

  I Why didn't Beethoven reinforce all the melody tones with chords?

  J What is the character of the theme? (Keep in mind tempo, harmony, scalewise melody, and even complementary phrase structure and dynamics.)

Example 19-9.   Schubert: "Ungeduld," from *Die schöne Müllerin*

EXERCISE 19-10

  A Circle all *nonchord* tones in Example 19-9.

  B On what beat (or part of the beat) in the measure is each nonchord tone placed?

  C What is the tone(s) before and after each nonchord tone(s)?

  D What is the function of each nonchord tone in the melody? Are the nonchord tones more or less tense than the tones that surround them?

  E Do any of these nonchord tones form into an extended chord? If so, which ones?

  F Do any of the nonchord tones form new chords within the melody that are not related to the supporting harmony?

RESULTS   Many nonchord tones appear on weak beats or on the weak part of a beat and move to a chord tone (Examples 19-7 and 19-8). Some nonchord tones appear on strong beats or on the strong part of a beat and move to a chord tone (Example 19-9).

Nonchord tones are melodic tones that are called *embellishments* or *nonessential tones*. These are tones that do not fit into the basic chord structure of the harmony. Such tones form into new chords or parts of chords that create new harmonic possibilities. They give the tonal melody a degree of independence and freedom from the basic chord structure, and enrich the melodic aspects of the texture.

Melody and its embellishment are the central focus in the nonharmonic music of the East. *Improvisation* in the form of melodic embellishment is an important aspect of twentieth-century jazz and seventeenth- and eighteenth-century Baroque music. (In the late Baroque, however, many of the embellishments were written out.)

A "blues" melody can be embellished in many ways with many extra nonchord tones (Example 19-10).

Example 19-10.   Blues embellishment

a.

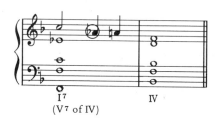

I⁷
(V⁷ of IV)   IV

b.

EXERCISE 19-11

Write a four-measure bass line, using only I$^{(7)}$, IV, and V$^{(7)}$ chords in root position. Then write a melodic line, using many nonchord tones.

To Sum Up   Nonchord tones give the melodic line a degree of independence from the basic harmony. They can appear in *any* line within the texture. They tend to highlight the melody or any part of it in which they appear, while they enrich the texture. They also tend to increase the level of dissonance, since a greater number of different tones sound at a specific time.

Nonchord tones are defined as such within the context of a tonal style in which the triad is the basic harmonic unit. In late tonal and nontonal music, nonchord tones could be considered essential parts of extended triads and/or complex chords.

PROJECT 19-3

A   Using the following "blues" bass, write a simple melody for instrument(s) and voice.

B   Write a variation of A, using nonchord tones to embellish it. Retain
the same bass.

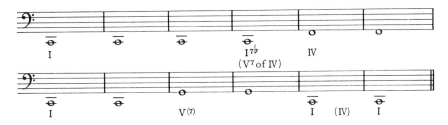

PROJECT 19-4

Write a short four-to-six-phrase instrumental piece with a simple
melody for voice or soprano instrument and piano or guitar. Support the
melody with primary and secondary triads and a clear cadence structure
after each phrase. Use the various cadences described in this chapter.

ANALYSIS 19-1

Study the first movement of Mozart's Piano Sonata, K. 331.

1   Compare the basic harmonic structure of variations 1–3 with that of
the theme.
2   Circle the melodic nonchord tones Mozart uses in the three variations.

LISTENING
SUGGESTIONS

Mozart: Piano Sonata, K. 331

Observe the variety of nonharmonic tones Mozart uses in each
variation. How does each of these tones contribute to the "character" of
the variation? What is the relation of tempo to the "character" of each
variation? Of harmony and tonality?

Bessie Smith: "Nobody's Blues but Mine" (Columbia G31093)

Observe how the vocalist "sings around" the chords with nonchord tones. Describe the "style."

20 LINES AND CHORDS IN TIME: Melodic, Harmonic, and Tonal Extensions in Tonal Style

OBJECTIVES

1. To *study* modulation in order to learn to extend and control melody, harmony, and tonality over larger spans of time.

2. To *write* pieces that incorporate the technique of modulation.

CAPSULE DEFINITION

Modulation　　Movement from one key center to another.

A. Modulation: Preliminary Explorations

Tonal melody and harmony are not restricted to a single scale and key, but can extend throughout the tonal system of related scales and keys. Because most of our music is limited to the twelve tones of the chromatic scale, these tones must serve a variety of melodic, harmonic, and tonal functions.

We know that melodic tones and chords can assume different "meanings" in different musical contexts. A chord that modulates from one key to another can "mean" one thing and have one function in the original key and "mean" something quite different and have another function in the new key. Exercise 20-1 explores the meaning and function of chords in the process of modulation.

EXERCISE 20-1

A   Analyze Examples 20-1–20-3.

B   Decide the key of each example. (Look at the key signature, and at the cadence if there is one.)

C   Place appropriate chord names and/or numbers under each chord.

D   Circle nonchord tones.

Example 20-1.   **J. S. Bach:** *"Gott sei uns gnädig and Barmherzig"* (chorale)

Example 20-2.   **J. S. Bach:** *French Suite No. 3*, minuet

Example 20-3.   **Beethoven:** *Piano Sonata,* Op. 2, No. 1, second movement, (mm. 20–22, 26–27)

RESULTS

Example 20-2 contains a modulation from B minor to D major. Example 20-3 is excerpted from the middle of the piece, and the passage is in "transition," moving harmonically from one key area to another.

However, in Example 20-1, Bach appears to create a tonally ambiguous situation. He does *not* establish a stable key area. The ambiguity is not fully resolved until the cadence in A major (measure 3).

In each example, the chord acts as a strong dominant (V or V⁷) that indicates the new tonic (I) and the new tonality. (See Examples 20-4–20-6).

Example 20-4.   Dominant-tonic modulation

Example 20-5.   Dominant-tonic modulation

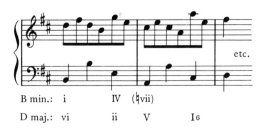

Example 20-6.   Dominant-tonic modulation

C maj.: V⁷   I   V⁷   I

The new tonality can be *transitory*, or it can be *established* as a new tonality with its related harmonies (IV–I–V, etc.). In Example 20-1, the melody and harmony move to a cadence in which A major is firmly established after two transitory modulations (F-sharp minor ⟶ A major ⟶ F-sharp minor).

B. Transitory Modulation: The Applied Dominant

A modulation from one key to another requires a clear harmonic progression of both the original and the new keys. The original key needs to be established before the movement to a new key can be felt as a modulation.

A composer may wish to move quickly through a series of keys, or he may want to stay in one key and *suggest* other keys. In either case, the new keys would not be firmly established and would not be felt as a true modulation. This form of modulation is called a *transitory modulation.*

In Example 20-1, the movement from F-sharp minor to A major back to F-sharp minor is made with a form of a dominant chord (V) to a tonic chord (I) in the new transitory key. Any *major* triad can act as a temporary dominant to another triad that can serve as a temporary tonic.

Exercises 20-2 and 20-3 explore various kinds of transitory modulations.

EXERCISE 20-2

A   Before each ascending scale tone in C major that will serve as the root of a temporary tonic chord, insert a tone that will act as the root of a temporary V or V.⁷

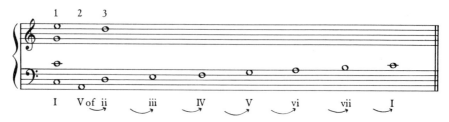

B   Play or sing the bass.

C   Harmonize the scale in four parts.

EXERCISE 20-3

Alter each secondary triad in Exercise 20-2 (ii, iii, vi, and vii) so that it could serve as a temporary V or V⁷ to a new inserted tonic (I). For example, ii with a raised third can serve as a temporary V to the real V, which acts as a temporary I:

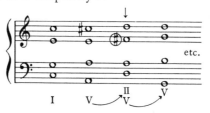

RESULTS

Any chord can serve as a new tonic in a new tonality. When the new tonic is temporary (that is, not firmly established with its related primary chords), it is not a true modulation. A chord that acts as a dominant (V or V⁷ and their inversions) to any temporary tonic (I) and its inversions (*any* primary or secondary chord in a key) is called an *applied* (or *secondary*) *dominant*.

Temporary modulations are important in extending the phrase internally. They also emphasize a particular chord within the key that can act as a temporary tonic.

In Example 20-7, the applied V moves directly to its "tonic," the V in F major. In Example 20-8, the applied V$\frac{6}{5}$ does *not* go to *its* "tonic" (the V in C major); instead, it goes to I$^6_4$. The applied V$^4_3$ does **go to** its "tonic," the V in C major, in the next measure.

Example 20-7.   **J. S. Bach:** *Little Notebook for Anna Magdalena Bach,* aria, m. 9

Example 20-8.   **Wagner:** *Tristan and Isolde,* prelude

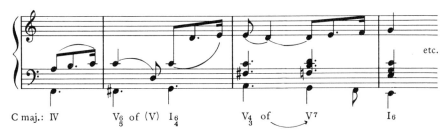

C maj.: IV   V$_5^6$ of (V) I$_4^6$ V$_3^4$ of $\longrightarrow$ V^7 I$_6$ etc.

C. Structural Modulation: Common Chords and Pivot Chords

A simple melody in a specific tonality with its accompanying harmonies usually lasts a short time. A melody with its accompanying harmonies that is extended either by transitory modulations and phrase extensions within a key or by modulation to other keys sets up larger time-expectations for its development, harmonically and tonally.

To modulate from one tonal area to another, we must determine the relationship between the chords of two keys. In Exercise 20-4, explore the relationships between chords in various keys.

EXERCISE 20-4

A   Write all the chords as simple primary and secondary triads in both keys (before and after the modulation) in Examples 20-1 and 20-2. Use both the major scale and the harmonic and melodic minor, ascending and descending to construct your chords.

B   What chords are common to both keys? Explain.

C   Write both keys under each example ($\begin{smallmatrix} \text{A major} \\ \text{F\# minor} \end{smallmatrix}$ etc.), and write the chord names and/or numbers as they apply to either or both keys.

RESULTS   In Example 20-1, the common chords are as follows:

A major: I   II   iii   IV   V   vi   vii

F# minor: iii(desc.mel.min.) iv   v   vi   vii(desc.mel.min.) I   ii

Examples 20-2 and 20-3 have the same major/relative-minor chord relationships: B minor/D major; D minor/F major.

All chords are related to some degree, given the flexibility of the minor scale in its various forms. The chords that are related most closely are:

Major:	II	VI	VII
Minor:	VI	I	ii

The reason for this close relationship is that these chords require no alteration.

Which chord in Examples 20-2 and 20-3 acts as the dominant (V) or modulating chord? Which of these chords do not relate to both keys, but only to the one to which it is going? In this case, a chord common to both keys is necessary as a transition or *pivot chord* that will connect both keys smoothly.

For a convincing modulation to be made, (1) the old key should be clearly established by the use of primary triads, (2) common chords should be used as pivot chords that lead from the old key to the dominant (V) of the new key, and (3) the new key should be clearly established with an eventual full cadence.

In Exercise 20-5, determine the chords that are common to both keys.

EXERCISE 20-5

In six or more chords, using the common chord as a pivot chord, modulate from:

A   C major to G major.
B   C major to F major.
C   C major to A minor.
D   C minor to A major.

Temporary and structural modulations can also be made without using the intermediary of a common chord and a dominant of the new key area.

1   Some modulations are "unprepared" and use no pivot chord (Example 20-9).
2   Others are made through chromatic alteration of a scale tone (Example 20-10).
3   Some are made through the use of one common tone (Example 20-11).
4   Others are made *enharmonically*—that is, through the use of a common chord or common tones that are spelled differently (Examples 20-12–20-14).

Example 20-9.   **Beethoven:** *Symphony No. 3,* first movement

Example 20-10.   **Brahms:** *Symphony No. 4,* third movement

Example 20-11.   **Beethoven:** *Symphony No. 8,* first movement

Example 20-12.   **Schumann:** *Widmung* from *Myrten,* Op. 25

Example 20-13.   **Schubert:** *"Ganymed,"* Op. 9, No. 3

A♭ maj.:   G♭ maj.: = F♯ maj.: - - - - - - - - - →E maj.:

Example 20-14.   **Schubert:** *"Die Junge Nonne,"* Op. 43, No. 1

F min.:   F maj.:

In each of Examples 20-9–20-14, the modulation is a shift in color as well as key.

EXERCISE 20-6

In less than six chords, and without using a common chord, modulate from:

A   D-flat major to C-sharp major.
B   E major to C major.
C   A minor to A major
D   C major to E-flat major.

Composers of the late nineteenth century used altered forms of the diatonic scales and the chromatic scale to modulate freely to related and distantly related keys in order to extend both the phrase and the piece. Wagner in particular used harmony as well as melody "melodically" to extend the line *in* a key—and then to repeat it sequentially in *another* key (Example 20-15).

Example 20-15.   **Wagner:** *Tristan and Isolde;* prelude: (a) mm. 32–34; (b) mm. 55–57

a.

b.

To Sum Up   Through melodic-harmonic and tonal extension, the structure of a piece can be extended in time.

A phrase can be extended harmonically by the use of transitory modulations through any chord that acts as an applied dominant to another chord in the key that acts as a temporary tonic.

A piece can be extended tonally, by the use of (1) modulation from one stable key area to a new key area by means of common chords, or (2) enharmonic "shifting" by means of differently spelled common tones or a common chord. Modulations can also be made through the use of a chromatically altered tone, one common tone, or no common tones or chords.

PROJECT 20-1

Take a simple melody you have written. Extend it through modulation, repeating a phrase or portion of a phrase sequentially on another pitch level and/or adding a complementary phrase. Harmonize the melody in three or four parts for instruments.

PROJECT 20-2

Take the melody of a Bach chorale. Harmonize it in four parts, placing the appropriate chord name and/or numerals under the bass.

PROJECT 20-3

Write an appropriate soprano part to the following bass. Then write inner parts. (Chords can be written in various positions.)

ANALYSIS 20-1

Analyze the chords in Example 20-16.

Example 20-16.   **Mozart:** *Piano Sonata*, K. 282, minuet

LISTENING
SUGGESTIONS

Wagner: *Tristan and Isolde*, prelude

Note the modulations *within* a key and the modulations to *other* key areas.

Schubert: "Erlkoenig"

Note the relationship between the modulations and the changes in mood.

Beethoven: Symphony No. 3, first movement

Note the themes and their relation to a key. Note the changes of key in the exposition, development, and recapitulation. Are the themes in the recapitulation in the same key as the themes in the exposition?

21 LINES AND CHORDS IN TIME: Melodic and Harmonic Extensions in Polytonal, Atonal, and Twelve-Tone Styles

OBJECTIVES

1. To *study* the tonal and nontonal melodic and harmonic extensions in the twentieth century.

2. To *write* pieces that incorporate the techniques of twentieth-century styles.

CAPSULE DEFINITIONS

Polyharmonic	More than one harmony at the same time.
Polytonal	More than one key at the same time.
Pedal tone	Usually, a low-held tone.
Sequence	Repetition on another pitch level.
Segment (segmentation)	A larger grouping of tones divided into smaller groups.
Permutation	A change in the order of tones.
Variation	An altering of one or more elements in a piece of music.

A. Polyharmonic and Polytonal Extensions

Many twentieth-century composers have evolved new uses of the tonal system that have transformed its sound and its function. Expanding their spatial world, they have extended chords *vertically* (complex chords, chord extensions), and their concept of tonality.

Chords that were once considered triadic extensions (see Chapter 10) are now considered to be two or more simultaneous triads that can function either *polyharmonically* in the same key or *polytonally* (that is, in two or more keys). In Example 21-1a, two harmonies are used simultaneously; in Example 21-1b, two keys are used simultaneously.

Example 21-1. **Milhaud:** *Creation du Monde*, modéré, (two excerpts)

a.

b.

Bb major
D major

Polyharmonies can also be found in pre-twentieth century music. Such polyharmonies result from:

1 a static pedal tone and moving harmonies (Example 21-2).
2 nonchord tones and the supporting harmonies (Example 21-3).

Example 21-2.   **J. S. Bach:** *"In dulce jubilo"*

Example 21-3.   **Beethoven:** *Violin Concerto*, first movement

Exercises 21-1 and 21-2 explore harmonic progressions of two simultaneous chords in the same key and then in different keys.

EXERCISE 21-1:
POLYHARMONIC
PROGRESSIONS

    A Divide six-tone extended triads into two triads *within* the same key in Exercise 10-3, separating them by an octave.

    B Play the triads.

    C Place the chord names and/or numbers below each triad.

    D Using these triads, write a polyharmonic progression, three voices per stave, each voice with its progression in which some of the polytriads share common tones.

EXERCISE 21-2:
POLYTONAL
PROGRESSIONS

    A Divide six-tone extended triads into two triads in *different* keys, separating them by an octave. As in a tonal modulation (in exercise 10-3), find those chords common to both keys.

    B Play the triads.

    C Place the chord names and/or numbers in each key below each triad.

    D Using the triads, write a polytonal progression, three voices per stave, each voice with its progressions in which the polyprogression can converge at one or more points on a chord common to both keys.

RESULTS   The sound of both exercises is "tonal," but the more distant the key relationship of each of the progressions, the greater the tonal conflict.

In some polyharmonic pieces a single harmony serves as a common chord, functioning polyharmonically in two or more key areas. The tones *within* the chord as well as the chord itself can assume a harmonic function.

In Example 21-4, the tone f serves as the seventh tone of the G chord and as a dominant root (V) of (B♭).

Example 21-4.   **Stravinsky:** *Symphonies of Wind Instruments*

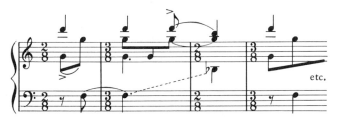

Because melodic tones also function harmonically, they can relate to more than one harmony or *key* in a polytonal style. In addition, the distinction between chord and nonchord tones becomes less clear.

EXERCISE 21-3

Example 21-5.   **Stravinsky:** *The Five Fingers*, No. 1

A   Play Example 21-5.
B   What key is it in?
C   Write a *simple* setting in tonal style.
D   What tones did you treat as nonchord tones?
E   Listen to and compare your version with the original piano version.
F   Compare the original piano version with Stravinsky's later instrumental version (Example 21-6).

Example 21-6.   **Stravinsky:** *Eight Instrumental Miniatures*

G   Write the chords as extended triads; circle the roots and mark their functions. For example:

H   Analyze the chords in Example 21-6 as polyharmonies. Circle probable root(s) and mark (name) their function. For example:

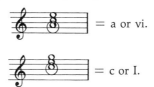

I   What tones in G and H are nonchord tones?

RESULTS   All the polyharmonic functions relate to the key *center* C. However, there is also a great deal of stress on the mediant e (iii) and the submediant a (vi) functions. This suggests the relative minor A, as well as C major.

This harmonic and tonal ambivalence is one of the elements that keeps one involved in the movement of the piece. The harmonies are also in close position and the instrumentation is "thick," both of which add to the tension of the piece. Note that not all the tones of a chord are present. Nor do they need to be present to suggest its harmonic function.

(Measure 3, E chord without the third g′)

In this sense, tones, intervals, and chords serve harmonic functions in a tonal or polytonal context. The most stable intervals (fifths and thirds) have clearer harmonic functions than those that are less stable (seconds and sevenths).

Exercise 21-4

Take any tonal melody you have written:

A   Write a piano version in which the melody tones function polyharmonically in the *same* key.
B   Write a four- or five-part choral version in which the melody tones function polyharmonically in two *different* keys.

RESULTS   With closely related keys, it is sometimes difficult to determine whether the tones and chords function in one key or more than one key.

Separating the registers of polyharmonies and the polykeys therefore becomes important if clear functions are desired. On another sound level, one that is beyond the notion of style and function, all sounds relate to one another in varying degrees. With many complex sound combinations, what is actually heard are fluctuating, massed chords that are distinguished from one another only by their relative position and dissonant character.

PROJECT 21-1

Write a free polytonal instrumental piece. Use the tones of two distantly related scales or keys for your melodic-harmonic material.

PROJECT 21-2

Take the melody of a Bach chorale. Set it for four or five parts in a polytonal style. Because you cannot use two different complete triads, have your melody tones function polyharmonically.

LISTENING
SUGGESTIONS

Stravinsky: Symphonies of Wind Instruments
Milhaud: *Création du Monde*
de Falla: Harpsichord Concerto

Observe the polyharmonies and their functions that combine into a composite sound.

Debussy: *Nocturnes:* "Nuages"

Observe the harmonies and the differences in sound between triadic extensions and polyharmonies.

ANALYSIS 21-1

Take either Stravinsky's Eight Instrumental Miniatures or his Five Fingers, No. 1.

A   Copy the complete melody and write a simple tonal setting.
B   Write a polyharmonic or polytonal version.
C   Compare your versions with that of Stravinsky.

B. Nontonal Extensions: Atonality

Many twentieth-century composers have rejected the tonal system. In its place they have evolved compositional procedures originally based on the chromatic scale. This scale, though used first in association with chromatic harmony and the expanded tonality of the late nineteenth century (as exemplified in the works of Wagner, Richard Strauss, and Mahler), was transformed in order to serve new sound concepts and functions. The elaboration and development of tonal materials (scales, chords, and their relationships) was abandoned, as was the resulting structure in various tonal forms.

The elaborate and sometimes lengthy nineteenth-century works became the dinosaurs of the early twentieth century. The "nontonal" composer relied essentially on a "nonsystem." This resulted in a music that was called *atonal*.

Since all tones were free to function independently, without reference to tonality, the composer had to find new methods of structuring a coherent musical composition. Most of the music of this period was terse, structurally concentrated, and dependent on minimal musical material.

In his *Six Little Piano Pieces*, Schoenberg used fragments consisting of melodic-rhythmic motives and interspersed these fragments with intervals and chords. (See Example 21-7.)

Exercise 21-7.   Schoenberg: *Six Little Piano Pieces*, Op. 19, No. 1

EXERCISE 21-5

    A Play or examine the soprano of Example 21-7; the bass; both together.

    B Mark the phrase structure; cadence structure.

    C What are the goal tones? How are they reached?

    D What intervals recur melodically and harmonically?

    E What chromatic tones are used in each measure?

F   Do some of these chromatic tones recur within the measure? Between the measures? In the soprano? In the bass? Between the soprano and bass?

G   Do you see or hear a chord or melodic fragment that suggests a triad or key?

H   Do any of the tones act as nonessential tones?

I   Describe the treatment of "rhythm."

RESULTS   As in tonal music, there are phrases and cadences in Example 21-7: the first phrase is located at the end of measure 1 (♪), the second at the end of measure 2 (♪). As in many tonal pieces, the two phrases are complementary, despite their brevity.

As in tonal music, small interval units act motivically to generate both the soprano (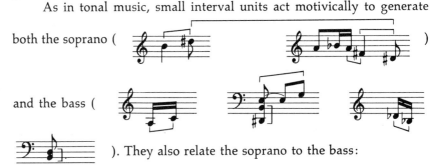)

and the bass (). They also relate the soprano to the bass:

Intervals of the minor second are used to extend the motive.

Elaboration and development is achieved through inversion and extension of motives, through the extension of the range, and through the addition of new material and phrases.

Finally, there is an *interdependence* between soprano and bass.

The composers who abandoned the tonal system, like the abstract artists, had a profound knowledge of the history and practice of their art. Schoenberg, Berg, and Webern, for example, all wrote successful pieces in late romantic styles before they changed to nontonal styles.

EXERCISE 21-6

Take any six, seven, or eight tones of the chromatic scale. Write a short melodic fragment or phrase. Use *any* of the twelve tones of the chromatic scale for a *minimal* accompaniment. (Use Example 21-7 as a model.)

C. Twelve-Tone Extensions

With the search for new and less restrictive means of expressing increasingly complex ideas, composers evolved a system in which the twelve chromatic tones could be arranged intervallically in a twelve-tone row that could be transposed to any of the pitch levels of the chromatic scales. The row could be stated in any of four ways:

1   the original form (O)—tones 1–12
2   the inverted form (I)—tones 1–12
3   the retrograde form (R)—tones 12–1
4   the retrograde-inverted form (RI)—tones 12–1

In this way, the language and musical gestures of the early atonal period were absorbed in the newer twelve-tone style. In one sense, the "new style" had to return to some of the principles of the tonal style so that it could expand structurally. Specifically, repetition (whether exact, sequential, augmented, diminished, inverted, retrograde, or fragmented), an important principle of *tonal* elaboration and development, was incorporated in the principle of constant variation—melodic, harmonic, and structural—of the twelve-tone row.

Example 21-8 illustrates the use of a twelve-tone row in which specific intervals are repeated throughout.

Example 21-8.   **Webern:** *Variations for Orchestra*

EXERCISE 21-7

A   Mark the interval structure of the twelve-tone row in Example 21-8.
B   What two intervals stand out in the row structure as a result of their repetition and their placement?
C   Mark those segments within the row that are related intervallically.
D   Invert the row.
E   Take six tones from Exercise 21-6. Add another six tones to complete an original twelve-tone row.

RESULTS   The row is based on two intervals—the minor second and the minor third. These are used *motivically* (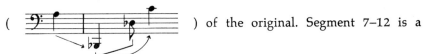)

throughout the row, which is segmented into groups of four and six tones. Stress tones depend on the position of the tones in the melody, and are emphasized through register, duration, dynamics, and instrumentation.

The retrograde form of the row is a transposed inversion ( ) of the original. Segment 7–12 is a transposed retrograde inversion of segment 1–6. Segment 9–12 is a transposed inversion of segment 1–4.

D. Segmentation and Permutation of the Row

One objection to the "classical" use of the twelve-tone row has been that originally, all twelve tones of the row *had* to be used—melodically and/or harmonically—before the row or another form of the row could be stated. Webern adhered strictly to this principle (see Examples 21-8 and 21-10). Schoenberg was somewhat more flexible in his treatment of the row (see Example 21-9).

1   The row can be segmented into two groups of six tones each, called *hexachords* (Examples 21-8 and 21-10).
2   The row can be segmented into groups of three or four tones each. (Example 21-10.)

Example 21-9.   **Schoenberg:** *Phantasy,* first movement, mm. 1–3

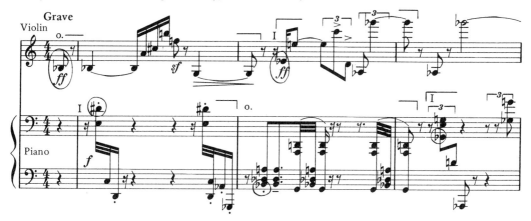

Example 21-10.   **Webern:** *Variations*

In his *Phantasy,* Schoenberg stated the *inversion* of the row (Example 21-9b) in the accompaniment, which is segment II of the melody (Example 21-9a). In measure 2, the melody states segment II against segment I in the accompaniment.

With the segmentation of the row, other ways of organizing the row became evident. Smaller segments of two, three, or four tones derived from the row could be grouped *sequentially* (1 2 3, 4 5 6, etc.) or *freely,* regardless of their original order. If the row is used freely, the composer has a wider range of choices available to him.

EXERCISE 21-8

    A   Using the tones of any row, freely construct segments of:

        1. two tones.

        2. three tones.

        3. four tones.

        4. a mixture of the above.

    B   Arrange each segment in A into an interval or chord.

Another way the row could be varied and extended is by *permutation*. With this method, one extends the row by grouping nonadjacent tones in various ways before going on to another form of the row—for example, 1 3 5 etc.

1 4 7 etc.

EXERCISE 21-9

    A Write at least five permutations of any row, extending each until you return to your starting number.

    B Arrange each group into three or more tone chords.

RESULTS

The number of tone combinations using one form of the row are limited. But if you combine various segments and permutations and transpose, invert, and retrograde them, you will find an endless chain of musical material and compositional possibilities.

E. Twelve-Tone-Row Linkage

In tonal music, melody and harmony can be varied and extended *within* the same key or scale by the progression of their tones, intervals, and chords. They can be varied *between* one key or scale and another by *modulation*.

In twelve-tone music, melody and harmony can be varied and extended within the same row form by the progression of their tones, intervals, and chords. They can be varied and extended between one row form and another on the same or a different pitch level by *row linkage*. Rows can be linked by:

    1 tones, intervals, and chords common to both rows that function like *pivot* chords in tonal music.

    2 tones, intervals, and chords that are *not* common to both rows.

Example 21-11.   Twelve-tone-row

Example 21-12.   **Dallapiccola:** *Quaderno Musicale di Annalibera*, No. 7

Example 21-13.   **Dallapiccola:** *Quaderno Musicale di Annalibera*, No. 1

Example 21-14.   **Schoenberg:** *Phantasy*, first movement

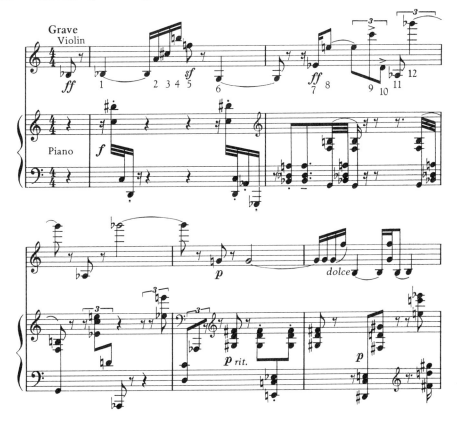

EXERCISE 21-10

A   Examine Examples 21-11–21-14.

B   Using the numbering of the tones in the original row (Examples 21-11, and 21-14), number the tones in each interval or chord in Examples 21-12–21-14.

C   How many intervals or chords did the composer derive from each form of the row?

D   In Examples 21-12–21-14, what are the tones, intervals, and chords that are common to the two forms of the row? If none, how are the rows linked?

E   Where are the cadence points in each example?

F   Compare Examples 21-12 and 21-13 with the original row (Example 21-11). Are they on the same pitch level, or were the rows in Examples 21-12 and 21-13 transposed?

G   What forms of the row are included in Examples 21-12–21-14?

RESULTS   In Examples 21-12 and 21-13, the two forms of the row are linked by common tones, intervals, and chords:

In Example 21-14, the two complete forms of the row are *not* linked by any common tones, intervals, or chords. The melody moves from g♭³ to g♮' to begin a retrograde version. The accompaniment moves from a quasi–G⁷ chord to a C major-minor third to begin an inversion of the original (the same form with which the accompaniment began).

To Sum Up   Any extended piece in a tonal, polytonal, atonal, or twelve-tone style requires musical materials (melodic, harmonic, and rhythmic) that can be developed through various forms of repetition and variation. Modulation in tonal and polytonal styles and transposition of the row in twelve-tone style in which there is either a change from key to key or from one form of the row to another are ways to extend and develop musical materials.

PROJECT 21-1

Write a short piece based on the tones of an original twelve-tone row, using only the original form of the row for your melody and harmony. (You can transpose and invert intervals and chords.)

PROJECT 21-2

Write a piece based on an original twelve-tone row, using various forms and transpositions of the row for your melody and harmony.

PROJECT 21-3

Write a piece based on an original twelve-tone row, using forms and transpositions of the row, including permutations of the row, for your melody and harmony.

ANALYSIS 21-1

Play or examine the four lines of Dallapiccola's *Quaderno Musicale Di Annalibera*, No. 1.

1   Describe the form (original, inverted, retrograde, or retrograde inversion) of each row repetition and its transposition.
2   Describe the melodic and harmonic use of the row.
3   Describe the phrase structure.
4   Describe the shape-form that evolves from the extension of the row.

LISTENING
SUGGESTIONS

Webern: Concerto, Op. 24
Stravinsky: *Fanfare for a New Theatre*
Powell: *Filigree Setting for String Quartet*

Observe the composers' use of row, row segments, pitched and nonpitched sounds, and fixed and free tempos.

22 CONCLUDING THOUGHTS

We return to our preliminary explorations of sound for a clue to present and future musical developments.

There are composers today who use traditional materials but organize them in their own ways. They make use of tonal and nontonal styles, combining them and/or expanding their usage in various ways. Others have either rejected the "traditional" styles or combined them with new musical materials that were not included in the original style and concept of sound.

Aleatoric music, which is based on chance and/or improvisation, can use musical materials that are related to twelve-tone music or musical materials that are totally independent. "Found" sounds—environmental, pitched and nonpitched, electronic, and taped sounds—can all be used as musical materials. In both cases, the style depends on choices that are *not* completely made by the composer. The performer must make choices as to how the given or "found" musical material is organized, using the composer's directions as a basis for these choices. This method (or "non-method") of musical composition is represented by such different individuals as Stockhausen and Cage.

Today, we can use very sophisticated machines, such as the Moog, Buckla, and Arp synthesizers, to produce and reproduce music. These machines have helped to broaden our concept of sound and have expanded our repertory of musical instruments. Although these new instruments can and have been used for composing music in various styles, each has unique sound possibilities that have stimulated composers to use sounds in new ways.

Musique concrète has combined instrumental and vocal sounds, "found" sounds, nonpitched sounds, and the technology of the tape machine. One important difference between this music and aleatory music is that the composer has made the compositional choices. The musical material is developed in many ways: it is recorded on tape, altered (speeded up, slowed down, etc.), spliced, and then arranged as a musical collage.

Electronic music produced on various types of electronic machines has expanded the spatial and temporal possibilities of music. Extremely high and low pitches and unusually fast speeds, impossible to achieve on the traditional instruments, can now be produced. Electronic music uses both traditional material, broadening the techniques of twelve-tone music, and a wide variety of pitched sounds. These sounds, combine various tempos, dynamics, and types and speeds of attack and decay. To vary the sound further, the composer can filter the frequencies to eliminate highs or lows.

Traditional instruments, their sounds, and the way these sounds are produced have undergone experimentation stimulated by the sound combinations of electronic instruments. Traditional instruments and voices have combined with the sounds of the tape and electronic machines to produce new sound combinations and new musical materials.

We are living in a period of musical extremes—"rock" music at one end of the popular music spectrum and avant-garde at the other end of the classical music spectrum. Whatever the style of music, it is important to recognize first those musical elements and materials that belong to that style. We must then determine how the composer organized these so as to shape a piece of music.

This book has presented the raw materials of music—how they can and have been used. If this knowledge can help you understand the music that has been and is being written, then the book has been useful. I hope it will stimulate you to explore these materials in greater depth.

BIBLIOGRAPHY: SECTION IV

Boulez, Pierre, *Boulez on Music Today*. Cambridge, Mass.: Harvard University Press, 1971.

Perle, George, *Serial Composition and Atonality*. Berkeley and Los Angeles: University of California Press, 1962.

Persichetti, Vincent, *Twentieth Century Harmony*. New York: Norton, 1961.

Reti, Rudolph, *Tonality, Atonality, Pantonality*. New York: Macmillan, 1958.

Rochberg, George, *The Hexachord and its Relation to the 12-Tone Row*. Theodore Presser, Bryn Mawr, Pa.: 1955.

Schoenberg, Arnold, *Structural Functions of Harmony*. New York: Norton, 1954.

———, *Style and Idea*. New York: Philosophical Library, 1950.

Strange, Allan, *Electronic Music*. Dubuque, Iowa: William C. Brown, 1973.

Vincent, John, *The Diatonic Modes in Modern Music*. New York, Mills, by arrangement with the California Press, Berkeley, 1951.

INDEX

245

INDEX OF
SELECTED MUSICAL EXAMPLES